CFA Level 3 2026 Core: Portfolio Management pathway, Private Markets pathway, and Private Wealth pathway

Azhar ul Haque Sario

Copyright

First Printing, 2025

Azhar.sario@hotmail.co.uk

ORCID: https://orcid.org/0009-0004-8629-830X
LinkedIn: https://www.linkedin.com/in/azharulhaquesario/

Disclaimer: This book is free from AI use. The cover was designed in Canva.

Disclaimer: This author has no affiliation with the CFA Institute. This publication is independently produced and is not endorsed by, sponsored by, or otherwise associated with the CFA Institute. CFA® is a registered trademark owned by the CFA Institute. This book is intended for educational purposes under the nominative fair use doctrine.

Contents

Section A: Core Topic

Chapter 1: Asset Allocation

Capital Market Expectations, Part 1: Framework and Macro Considerations

The Role and Framework of Capital Market Expectations

Capital market expectations are the essential building blocks for managing investment portfolios. Think of them as the informed guesses that investors and portfolio managers make about how different investments will perform in the future. These aren't just random predictions; they are calculated estimates of the risk and return for various asset classes, like stocks, bonds, and real estate. The primary role of these expectations is to guide the strategic asset allocation process. This is the crucial step where a manager decides how to divide a portfolio among different assets to achieve the investor's long-term goals. Without a solid set of expectations, you would just be guessing where to put your money.

A solid framework for developing these expectations is systematic and disciplined. It starts with specifying the set of asset classes to be included and the time horizon for the forecast—are we looking one year ahead or ten? The framework then involves a deep dive into historical data, but with a critical eye, understanding that the past doesn't always predict the future. Next, it requires identifying the valuation models and methods that will be used to forecast returns. This could involve anything from simple dividend discount models for stocks to more complex econometric models. The final step is to document the process and the conclusions, allowing for transparency and periodic review. This structured approach ensures that the resulting expectations are objective, consistent, and defensible, forming a reliable foundation for building robust portfolios.

Challenges in Developing Capital Market Forecasts

Forecasting the future of capital markets is notoriously difficult, and anyone who tells you otherwise is probably selling something. One of the biggest challenges is simply the sheer number of variables at play. Markets are influenced by everything from geopolitical events and technological disruptions to shifts in consumer sentiment and corporate scandals. The world is a complex, interconnected system, and financial markets are its hyperactive nerve center. Trying to model all these moving parts with perfect accuracy is practically impossible. The data we rely on can also be a minefield. Financial data is often "noisy," meaning it contains a lot of random fluctuations that can obscure underlying trends. Historical data can also be misleading, as the structure of the economy and markets changes over time. What worked in the 1980s might not work today.

Another significant hurdle is the human element. We are all susceptible to a range of behavioral biases. For example, the "analyst trap" can lead forecasters to become overly attached to their existing models, even when new evidence suggests they are flawed. We might extrapolate recent trends too far into the future, a bias known as recency bias, or become overly optimistic or pessimistic based on the current mood of the market. There's also the problem of "black swan" events—unforeseeable, high-impact occurrences that no model could have predicted. Finally, there's the simple fact that models are, by their very nature, simplifications of reality. They are based on assumptions, and if those assumptions turn out to be wrong, the forecast will be wrong too. It's a constant battle between seeking precision and acknowledging uncertainty.

Exogenous Shocks and Economic Growth Trends

Exogenous shocks are the curveballs that life throws at the global economy. These are sudden, unexpected events that originate outside the normal functioning of the economy, yet they can have a profound impact on its trajectory. Think of things like the global pandemic in 2020, a major war, a sudden spike in oil prices due to a natural disaster, or a groundbreaking technological invention. These shocks can hit both the supply side and the demand side of the economy. A pandemic, for instance, disrupts supply chains and forces businesses to close (a supply shock), while also causing consumers to stay home and spend less (a demand shock).

The effect of these shocks on economic growth trends can be immediate and long-lasting. In the short term, a negative shock will almost certainly push an economy into a slowdown or recession. However, the long-term impact is more complex. A shock might permanently lower the potential growth rate of an economy by destroying capital or reducing the labor force. But shocks can also be positive catalysts. The internet, for example, was an exogenous technological shock that fundamentally reshaped industries and unleashed decades of productivity growth. Understanding these shocks is critical for forecasters because they force a re-evaluation of the baseline assumptions about how an economy will grow over time, which in turn affects expectations for corporate earnings and investment returns.

Applying Economic Growth Trend Analysis

Analyzing the long-term trend of economic growth is fundamental to forming capital market expectations. The potential growth rate of an economy—the speed at which it can grow without stoking inflation—is a key determinant of the overall return available from its financial markets. This trend growth is primarily driven by two things: the growth in the labor force and the growth in labor productivity. If a country's population is aging and its workforce is shrinking, its potential growth rate will naturally decline unless it can find a way to make each worker dramatically more productive.

This analysis directly feeds into forecasts for different asset classes. For equities, the long-term trend in GDP growth provides a ceiling for the aggregate growth of corporate earnings. It's hard for company profits to consistently grow much faster than the economy itself over the long run. For bonds, the trend growth rate influences expectations for inflation and, consequently, the level of interest rates. A higher growth economy can typically support higher real interest rates. For real estate, economic growth drives demand for both commercial and residential properties, influencing rental income and property values. By grounding capital market forecasts in a realistic assessment of long-term economic potential, investors can avoid making overly optimistic assumptions and build more resilient portfolios.

Major Approaches to Economic Forecasting

There are several ways to peer into the economic future, each with its own strengths and weaknesses. One major approach is econometric modeling. This is the most quantitative method, using statistical techniques and historical data to build complex models with dozens or even hundreds of equations that describe the relationships between variables like inflation, interest rates, and GDP growth. These models are great for running "what-if" scenarios, but they can be rigid and often fail to predict major turning points because they are based on past relationships.

Another approach is using leading economic indicators. This method focuses on tracking a handful of economic variables that have historically tended to rise or fall before the rest of the economy does. Things like building permits, stock market prices, and initial jobless claims are classic examples. It's a simpler, more intuitive approach, but it can give false signals, and the lead time can be inconsistent. A third method is the checklist approach, which is more qualitative. A forecaster might analyze a wide range of data points and conditions, from monetary policy to consumer confidence, essentially ticking boxes to arrive at a judgment about where the economy is headed. It's flexible and can incorporate a wide array of information, but it's also highly subjective and depends heavily on the skill of the forecaster. Often, the best approach is a pragmatic one that combines elements from all of these methods.

Business Cycles and Their Effect on Expectations

The economy doesn't grow in a straight line; it moves in waves, known as the business cycle. This cycle has distinct phases: expansion (when the economy is growing), the peak (the high point), contraction or recession (when the economy is shrinking), and the trough (the low point). Understanding where we are in this cycle is crucial because it has a huge impact on investment performance, affecting both short-term and long-term expectations.

In the short term, the business cycle is a dominant driver of asset returns. During an expansion, corporate profits are rising, and unemployment is falling. This is usually a fantastic environment for stocks and a tougher one for safe-haven government bonds. As the economy approaches its peak, however, things can get tricky. Inflation might start to rise, prompting the central bank to raise interest rates, which can be bad for both stocks and bonds. During a recession, the opposite happens. Stocks tend to perform poorly as earnings plummet, while government bonds often rally as investors seek safety and central banks cut interest rates to stimulate growth. Over the long term, the business cycle's influence is smoothed out, but the cumulative returns achieved through these cycles shape the long-term result. A manager might adjust their portfolio's risk level based on their assessment of the current phase of the business cycle.

The Relationship Between Inflation and the Business Cycle

Inflation and the business cycle are locked in an intricate dance. Inflation measures the rate at which the general level of prices for goods and services is rising, and its behavior is closely tied to the economy's booms and busts. During the expansion phase of the business cycle, as demand for goods and services heats up and the labor market tightens, inflationary pressures typically build. Companies find it easier to raise prices, and workers can demand higher wages. This inflation tends to accelerate as the economy nears its peak.

Conversely, during a recession, demand slumps. Businesses are forced to compete for fewer customers, often by cutting prices or offering discounts. Unemployment rises, reducing workers' bargaining power for higher wages. This environment is disinflationary (a slowing of the inflation rate) or even deflationary (falling prices). For investors, this relationship has profound implications. Cash becomes more attractive when inflation is falling, as its purchasing power is preserved. Bonds, especially those with fixed interest payments, are hurt by unexpected inflation because it erodes the real value of their returns. Equities have a more complex relationship; moderate inflation can be good for stocks as it allows companies to increase prices, but high and volatile inflation is often negative as it creates uncertainty and can squeeze profit margins. Real estate, as a real asset, often performs well during inflationary periods as property values and rents tend to rise with the general price level.

The Effects of Monetary and Fiscal Policy

Governments and central banks are not passive observers of the business cycle; they actively try to manage it using monetary and fiscal policy. Monetary policy is wielded by a country's central bank (like the U.S. Federal Reserve). Its primary tools are interest rates and control over the money supply. When the economy is overheating and inflation is a concern, the central bank will raise interest rates to make borrowing more expensive, which cools down spending and investment. When the economy is in a recession, it will cut interest rates to encourage borrowing and stimulate activity. The goal is to smooth out the peaks and troughs of the cycle, aiming for stable growth and low inflation.

Fiscal policy is controlled by the government and involves its spending and taxation powers. To fight a recession, the government can engage in expansionary fiscal policy by increasing its spending (e.g., on infrastructure projects) or by cutting taxes to leave more money in the pockets of consumers and businesses. This directly injects demand into the economy. To cool down an overheating economy, it can use contractionary fiscal policy by cutting spending or raising taxes. Both monetary and fiscal policy have lags—it takes time for their effects to be fully felt—and their effectiveness can be debated, but they are powerful forces that investors must watch closely as they directly influence economic conditions and market behavior.

The Yield Curve as an Economic Predictor

The yield curve is a simple graph that plots the interest rates (or yields) of bonds having equal credit quality but different maturity dates. Typically, a bond with a longer maturity will have a higher yield to compensate investors for tying up their money for a longer period. This results in a "normal" upward-sloping yield curve. However, the shape of this curve can change, and those changes are watched by economists and investors as a powerful predictor of future economic activity.

A steepening yield curve, where long-term rates are rising faster than short-term rates, often signals that investors expect stronger economic growth and higher inflation in the future. But the most famous signal comes from an inverted yield curve. This occurs when short-term yields are higher than long-term yields. This unusual shape suggests that investors are worried about the near-term future. They expect the central bank to be cutting interest rates down the road to fight off a recession. Historically, an inverted yield curve has been one of the most reliable predictors of an upcoming recession. The curve's shape is heavily influenced by policy. Monetary policy directly sets the short-term end of the curve, while expectations about future growth, inflation, and fiscal policy (which affects the supply of government bonds) all shape the long-term end.

Macroeconomic Linkages Between Economies

In today's globalized world, no economy is an island. The macroeconomic linkages between countries are powerful and complex, meaning that an event in one part of the world can quickly ripple across the globe. One of the most important linkages is international trade. A booming economy in China, for example, increases its demand for raw materials from Brazil and machinery from Germany, boosting growth in those countries. A recession in the United States reduces its consumer spending, hurting exports from Mexico and Vietnam.

Interest rates and exchange rates are also crucial channels. If the U.S. Federal Reserve raises interest rates, it can attract capital from all over the world as investors seek higher returns. This flow of capital strengthens the U.S. dollar, which makes U.S. exports more expensive and imports cheaper. This can affect the trade balance and the competitiveness of domestic industries. For emerging market countries, a stronger dollar can make it more expensive to pay back debt that is denominated in U.S. dollars. These interconnected financial flows mean that portfolio managers can't just focus on their home country; they must maintain a global perspective to understand the risks and opportunities facing their investments.

Capital Market Expectations, Part 2: Forecasting Asset Class Returns

Setting Expectations for Fixed-Income Returns

Forecasting returns on fixed-income securities, like bonds, is a little more straightforward than for stocks because the basic components are known from the start. A bond's return comes from its yield and any change in its price.

The most fundamental building block is the yield-to-maturity (YTM). For an investor who buys a bond and holds it until it matures, the YTM is a very good estimate of the return they will receive. It accounts for all the coupon payments and the difference between the purchase price and the bond's face value. So, if you're planning to hold a bond for its entire life, the current YTM is your best friend for forecasting.

However, things get more complicated if you don't plan to hold the bond to maturity. The price of a bond can, and does, change. The main driver of these price changes is shifts in interest rates. If interest rates in the market go up, newly issued bonds will offer higher yields, making your older, lower-yield bond less attractive. Its price will have to fall to compete. Conversely, if interest rates fall, your bond's price will rise. This relationship means that a key part of forecasting fixed-income returns is forecasting the direction of interest rates.

Another way to think about this is by breaking down the expected return into its core parts:

The Risk-Free Rate: This is the return you'd get on a super-safe investment, like a U.S. Treasury bond. It's the base layer for all other returns.

Inflation Expectations: Lenders demand to be compensated for the fact that the money they get back in the future will be worth less due to inflation. So, expected inflation is a big piece of the expected return.

Spreads: For any bond that isn't a government bond (like corporate bonds), there's an extra layer of risk. The company could go out of business and fail to pay you back. This is called credit risk. The extra yield you get for taking on this risk is called a "credit spread." So, for a corporate bond, you need to forecast not only interest rates but also whether you think these spreads will widen (get bigger) or tighten (get smaller).

A simple model for forecasting a bond's return over a short period, say one year, is:

Expected Return = Yield Income + Rolldown Return - Expected Price Change

Yield Income is the coupon payment you receive.

Rolldown Return comes from the fact that as a bond gets closer to maturity, its price naturally "rolls down" the yield curve.

Expected Price Change is your best guess about how interest rates will move.

In essence, setting expectations for fixed-income is about understanding the current yield and then making an educated guess about how interest rates and credit conditions will change.

Risks and Analysis of Emerging Market Fixed-Income

Investing in the bonds of emerging market countries can be very attractive because they often offer much higher yields than bonds from developed countries. But with high potential reward comes high risk.

One of the biggest risks is sovereign risk, which is the risk that a national government will default on its debt. This can happen for many reasons: political instability, economic collapse, or even a simple unwillingness to pay. When a country defaults, investors can lose a huge portion of their investment.

Another major risk is currency risk. Many emerging market bonds are issued in their local currency. If that currency weakens against your home currency (say, the U.S. dollar), then the returns you get will be worth less when you convert them back. Emerging market currencies can be incredibly volatile, swinging wildly due to political news or changes in commodity prices.

Liquidity risk is also a concern. In a crisis, it might be difficult to sell your emerging market bonds without taking a big loss because there aren't many buyers.

To evaluate these risks, analysts use country risk analysis. This involves a deep dive into the country's health, looking at several factors:

Political Stability: Is the government stable? Are there risks of coups, civil unrest, or major policy shifts that could harm foreign investors? Analysts look at things like the rule of law, corruption levels, and the predictability of the political process.

Economic Strength: How healthy is the economy? Analysts examine GDP growth rates, inflation, and unemployment. A country with a diverse, growing economy is less likely to default than one that relies on a single commodity.

Fiscal Health: How responsible is the government with its finances? This involves looking at the level of government debt as a percentage of GDP, the budget deficit, and the country's history of paying its debts.

External Position: How does the country interact with the rest of the world? Analysts look at the country's balance of payments, its level of foreign exchange reserves (which it can use to pay foreign debts), and its overall reliance on foreign capital.

By scoring a country on these different metrics, analysts can build a picture of its overall creditworthiness and decide if the high yield is worth the associated risks.
Setting Expectations for Equity Market Returns

Forecasting equity returns is much harder than for bonds because there are so many more uncertainties. Stocks don't have a maturity date or promised coupon payments. Their returns come from dividends and capital appreciation (the stock price going up).

There are a few major approaches to this challenge.

The Dividend Discount Model (DDM): This is a classic approach. The idea is that the price of a stock is the present value of all its future dividends. To forecast the return for the whole market, you can use a version of this model. The expected return is roughly equal to the dividend yield plus the expected growth rate of dividends. So, if the market's dividend yield is 2% and you expect dividends to grow at 5% per year, your expected return is about 7%. The hard part, of course, is accurately forecasting that growth rate.

The Grinold-Kroner Model: This is a more detailed version of the DDM. It breaks down the expected return into several components:

Dividend Yield: Same as before.

Inflation: The portion of earnings growth that just comes from rising prices.

Real Earnings Growth: The true, inflation-adjusted growth of company profits.

Repurchasing Yield: The effect of companies buying back their own stock, which reduces the number of shares and boosts earnings per share.

Change in P/E Ratio: This is the speculative component. It reflects whether you think the market will become more or less expensive. If you expect the Price-to-Earnings (P/E) ratio to increase, that adds to your expected return.

The Equity Risk Premium (ERP) Approach: This method builds up the expected return from the bottom. It starts with the risk-free rate and adds an extra return that investors demand for taking on the risk of investing in stocks.

Expected Equity Return = Risk-Free Rate + Equity Risk Premium

The ERP is not constant; it changes over time. It tends to be higher when investors are fearful and the economy is struggling, and lower when investors are optimistic.

Forecasting the ERP involves looking at historical averages, economic conditions, and investor sentiment.

Each of these methods has its strengths and weaknesses, and analysts often use a combination of them to arrive at a reasonable forecast.

Risks of Investing in Emerging Market Equities

Much like with emerging market bonds, investing in their stock markets offers the potential for high growth but comes with a unique set of significant risks.

Corporate governance is a huge one. In many emerging markets, the rules protecting minority shareholders are weak. There might be a risk that the company is run for the benefit of a controlling family or the government, not for all shareholders. It can be harder to get reliable financial information, and accounting standards may not be as rigorous.

Political and regulatory risk is also elevated. A sudden change in government policy, the nationalization of an industry, or restrictions on taking money out of the country can have a devastating impact on stock prices. Property rights might not be as secure as they are in developed countries.

Currency risk is just as important for equities as it is for bonds. A falling local currency will reduce the value of your stock holdings and any dividends you receive.

Finally, market efficiency can be a double-edged sword. Emerging markets are often less efficient, meaning prices may not always reflect all available information. This can create opportunities for savvy investors to find undervalued companies, but it also means that markets can be more volatile and prone to bubbles and crashes.

Investors in these markets need to be prepared for a much bumpier ride.

Economic and Competitive Factors in Real Estate

Real estate is a unique asset class, and its returns are driven by a specific set of factors that blend broad economic trends with very local, competitive dynamics.

On the economic side, real estate is highly sensitive to the business cycle.

GDP Growth: A strong, growing economy means lower unemployment and rising incomes. This directly fuels demand for all types of property. Businesses expand, so they need more office and industrial space. People have more money, so they can afford to rent more expensive apartments or buy homes. Retailers see more foot traffic, boosting demand for shop space.

Interest Rates: Real estate is often purchased with borrowed money, so the level of interest rates is critical. Lower rates make mortgages and commercial loans cheaper, which stimulates demand and pushes property values up. Higher rates have the opposite effect.

Demographics: Long-term trends like population growth, an aging population, or shifts in household size can have a massive impact. For example, a growing population in a city will increase demand for housing, while an aging population might boost demand for healthcare-related properties.

On the competitive side, real estate is all about "location, location, location."

Local Supply and Demand: The most important factor is the balance between the amount of available property in a specific area and the number of people or businesses who want to use it. A city with many new office buildings under construction (high supply) but weak job growth (low demand) will likely see falling rents and property values.

Sector-Specific Trends: Different types of real estate face different competitive pressures. The rise of e-commerce has been a huge boon for industrial warehouses but has created immense challenges for traditional shopping malls. The shift to remote work is changing the entire landscape for office buildings.

Barriers to Entry: Is it easy to build a new property in a certain area? High barriers, such as tough zoning laws or a lack of available land, can limit new supply and keep values high for existing properties.

Forecasting real estate returns requires a two-level analysis: a top-down view of the economy and a bottom-up understanding of the competitive dynamics in a specific location and property sector.

Major Approaches to Forecasting Exchange Rates

Forecasting how currencies will move against each other is notoriously difficult, but there are several theories that provide a framework.

Purchasing Power Parity (PPP): This is the long-run anchor. The idea is that a basket of goods should cost the same in two different countries after you account for the exchange rate. If a basket of goods costs $100 in the U.S. and €120 in Europe, PPP implies the exchange rate should be $1 = €1.20. If the actual exchange rate is different, the theory suggests it will eventually move toward the PPP rate. In the short term, however, exchange rates can deviate from PPP for years.

Interest Rate Parity: This theory connects exchange rates to interest rates. It suggests that the difference in interest rates between two countries should be equal to the expected change in their exchange rate. For example, if interest rates are 5% in the U.S. and 2% in Japan, this theory predicts that the Japanese yen will appreciate against the dollar by about 3% over the next year to offset the lower interest rate. This prevents investors from making risk-free money simply by moving capital from one country to another.

The Balance of Payments Approach: This focuses on the flow of money into and out of a country. A country with a large current account surplus (exporting more than it imports) will see a high demand for its currency, causing it to strengthen. Conversely, a country with a large deficit needs to constantly attract foreign capital, which can put downward pressure on its currency.

Monetary and Asset Market Models: These models view exchange rates as prices of an asset (money). They look at factors like money supply growth, inflation expectations, and real interest rate differentials to forecast currency movements. For instance, a country that is rapidly increasing its money supply is likely to see its currency depreciate.

In practice, no single model works perfectly. Most forecasters use a combination of these approaches, looking at long-run fundamentals like PPP while also considering short-term capital flows and interest rate differentials.

Methods of Forecasting Volatility

Volatility—the magnitude of price swings in an asset—is not constant. It comes in waves, with periods of calm followed by periods of turbulence. Forecasting volatility is crucial for risk management and asset allocation.

One of the simplest methods is to use historical volatility. This involves looking at the standard deviation of returns over some past period (e.g., the last 30 days) and assuming that the near future will be similar. While simple, this method is often too reactive and doesn't capture changes in the market environment very well.

A more sophisticated approach is to use time-series models, such as the ARCH (Autoregressive Conditional Heteroskedasticity) and GARCH (Generalized ARCH) models. These models are based on two key observations about market volatility:

Volatility Clustering: High-volatility periods tend to be followed by more high-volatility periods, and low-volatility periods are followed by more low-volatility periods.

Mean Reversion: Volatility tends to revert to a long-run average over time.

GARCH models use recent information about market returns and volatility to forecast the next period's volatility. They have proven to be quite effective in capturing the short-term dynamics of volatility.

Another powerful source of information is implied volatility. This is the volatility that is "implied" by the prices of options. Options traders make bets on the future volatility of an asset, and their collective wisdom is baked into the option's price. By reverse-engineering an options pricing model, we can extract the market's consensus forecast for volatility. For example, the VIX index is a well-known measure of the implied volatility of the S&P 500. Implied volatility is often considered the best forecast of volatility over the life of the option.

Recommending and Justifying Portfolio Changes

Strategic asset allocation is about setting long-term weights for different asset classes. But investors can also make tactical adjustments based on expected changes in the macroeconomic environment.

The process involves first forecasting key macroeconomic factors and then thinking through how those factors will affect the relative performance of different asset classes.

Let's consider an example. Suppose your analysis leads you to believe that global economic growth is about to accelerate.

Justification: You might see leading economic indicators turning up, rising consumer confidence, and expansionary fiscal policy in major countries.

Impact on Asset Classes:

Equities: Stronger growth is great for corporate profits, so you would expect equities to perform well. Cyclical sectors, like industrials and consumer discretionary, should do particularly well. Emerging market equities, which are highly sensitive to global growth, would also be attractive.

Fixed-Income: Strong growth often leads to higher inflation and prompts central banks to raise interest rates. Both of these are bad for government bond prices. Corporate bonds might do okay because the stronger economy reduces default risk, but they would still face headwinds from rising rates.

Real Estate: Would likely benefit from higher demand for space and rising rents.

Recommended Changes: Based on this outlook, you would recommend increasing the weight of equities in the portfolio, perhaps with a specific tilt toward emerging markets and cyclical stocks. At the same time, you would recommend reducing the weight of government bonds, especially those with long maturities, as they are most sensitive to interest rate increases.

Now, consider the opposite scenario: you expect a recession.

Justification: You might see an inverted yield curve, falling business investment, and weakening labor markets.

Impact on Asset Classes:

Equities: Would be expected to perform poorly as corporate earnings fall.

Fixed-Income: In a recession, central banks typically cut interest rates to stimulate the economy. This would cause high-quality government bond prices to rise, making them a safe haven.

Recommended Changes: You would recommend reducing the allocation to equities and increasing the allocation to long-term government bonds.

The key is to have a clear, well-reasoned view on the future path of the economy and to understand the historical relationships between macroeconomic factors and asset class returns. Every recommendation must be justified by a sound analysis of the changing economic landscape.

Overview of Asset Allocation

An Overview of Asset Allocation

Asset allocation is the cornerstone of building a successful investment portfolio. It's not about picking individual winning stocks or trying to time the market. Instead, it's about strategically dividing your investment capital among different asset categories, like stocks, bonds, real estate, and cash. The goal is to balance risk and reward by diversifying your holdings according to your personal goals, risk tolerance, and investment timeline. A well-thought-out asset allocation strategy is one of the most significant factors determining your long-term investment returns. This guide will walk you through the essential elements, from the governance that underpins a strategy to the practical choices of rebalancing.

1. Effective Investment Governance and Its Role in Asset Allocation

Think of investment governance as the rulebook for managing money. It's the framework of people, policies, and processes put in place to ensure that investment decisions are made thoughtfully and effectively. A strong governance structure is the foundation of any sound asset allocation strategy. One of the primary elements is a well-defined set of long-term investment objectives. What is the portfolio trying to achieve? Is it growth, income, or capital preservation?

Clear roles and responsibilities are also crucial. Who has the authority to make decisions? Who is responsible for monitoring the portfolio? This avoids confusion and ensures accountability. Perhaps the most critical document in investment governance is the Investment Policy Statement

(IPS). The IPS is a formal document that outlines the entire investment strategy. It details the objectives, the constraints (like liquidity needs or ethical considerations), and the strategic asset allocation itself. It also specifies the process for monitoring performance and the rules for rebalancing the portfolio. This document acts as a guidepost, keeping the investment strategy on track through market ups and downs and preventing emotional, reactive decisions. Without good governance, an asset allocation plan is just a hopeful wish; with it, it becomes a disciplined, robust strategy.

2. The Economic Balance Sheet: A Holistic View for Asset Allocation

A traditional balance sheet lists your financial assets (stocks, bonds, cash) and liabilities (mortgages, loans). An economic balance sheet, however, gives a much fuller and more realistic picture of your financial situation. It expands the definition of both assets and liabilities to include things that don't show up on a typical financial statement.

On the asset side, the most significant addition is often human capital. This represents the present value of your future earnings potential. A young doctor has very high human capital, which is relatively stable and bond-like. A professional athlete, on the other hand, might have high but more volatile and stock-like human capital due to a shorter career span. The economic balance sheet also includes the present value of future pension benefits or other entitlements.

On the liability side, it includes the present value of all your future consumption goals. This isn't just about paying off a mortgage; it's about funding retirement, paying for children's education, and covering healthcare costs. By looking at this complete picture, an investor can make much smarter asset allocation decisions. For example, an individual with high, stable human capital can afford to take on more risk in their financial portfolio. Conversely, someone approaching retirement with most of their liabilities in the near future needs a more conservative allocation. This holistic view ensures that your asset allocation is truly aligned with your entire life's financial landscape.

3. Comparing Investment Objectives: Asset-Only, Liability-Relative, and Goals-Based

Not all investment strategies are trying to achieve the same thing. The objectives can be broadly categorized into three different approaches: asset-only, liability-relative, and goals-based. Each has a distinct focus that shapes the entire asset allocation process.

The asset-only approach is the most traditional. Its primary objective is to maximize the portfolio's risk-adjusted return, often without explicit consideration for any specific liabilities. The focus is on the assets themselves. Performance is typically measured against a market benchmark, like the S&P 500. This approach is common for endowments or individual investors who are purely focused on wealth accumulation. The main game here is growing the pot of money as efficiently as possible.

The liability-relative approach, in contrast, is all about funding future obligations. The primary objective is to ensure the portfolio has sufficient assets to cover its liabilities. This is the world of pension funds and insurance companies. Their success isn't measured by beating the market, but by their ability to make future payments. The asset allocation is constructed specifically to match the characteristics of the liabilities, such as their duration and cash flow needs.

Finally, the goals-based approach is a more personal and increasingly popular method. It frames investing around achieving specific life goals, like buying a house, funding a child's college education, or securing a comfortable retirement. The portfolio is often divided into distinct sub-portfolios, each with its own asset allocation tailored to a specific goal's time horizon and importance. The main objective is to maximize the probability of achieving each of these goals.

4. Contrasting Concepts of Risk: A Different Lens for Each Approach

Just as the objectives differ, the way risk is defined and measured also changes dramatically depending on the investment approach. What one strategy considers risky, another might see as perfectly acceptable. It's all about perspective.

In the asset-only world, risk is almost always defined as the volatility of returns, typically measured by standard deviation. The big fear is watching the market value of your portfolio fluctuate wildly. A "risky" asset is one with a high standard deviation, like an emerging market stock. The goal of diversification in this context is to build a portfolio with the highest expected return for a given level of volatility. The conversation is dominated by Sharpe ratios and tracking error.

For a liability-relative investor, the concept of risk is completely different. The primary risk isn't volatility; it's shortfall risk. This is the danger that the assets will be insufficient to meet the liabilities. A pension fund manager isn't losing sleep over a 10% dip in the stock market if their assets are still comfortably above their future obligations. Their nightmare is a scenario where interest rate changes cause the value of their liabilities to grow faster than their assets. Therefore, a "risky" asset isn't necessarily a volatile one, but one that is poorly correlated with the liabilities they need to fund.

In a goals-based framework, risk takes on a much more personal meaning. The ultimate risk is the failure to achieve a specific life goal. For the goal of funding college in five years, the risk is not having enough money when the tuition bill arrives. For the retirement goal, the risk is outliving your money. Volatility matters, but only in how it impacts the probability of reaching that goal. An investor might be perfectly comfortable with short-term volatility in their long-term retirement bucket, but would want to eliminate it completely for a down payment they need to make next year.

5. Asset Classes: The Building Blocks for Managing Systematic Risk

Systematic risk refers to the broad market risks that affect all investments and cannot be eliminated through diversification. Think of things like interest rate changes, inflation, and economic recessions. You can't diversify these away, but you can manage your exposure to them. This is where asset classes come in. Asset classes are groups of securities that exhibit similar characteristics, behave similarly in the marketplace, and are subject to the same laws and regulations.

Each asset class provides a different exposure to systematic risk factors. For example, equities (stocks) are highly sensitive to economic growth risk. When the economy is booming, stocks tend to do well. Bonds, on the other hand, are highly sensitive to interest rate and inflation risk. When inflation unexpectedly rises, the value of most bonds falls. By combining different asset classes in a portfolio, an investor can balance these exposures.

To be considered a legitimate asset class, a group of assets should meet several criteria. First, the assets within the class should be homogenous, meaning they are reasonably similar. Second, the asset classes themselves should be mutually exclusive; an asset shouldn't be able to fit into two different classes. Third, the asset class should be diversified, so the performance isn't just driven by one or two securities. Finally, the asset class should represent a meaningful portion of global wealth and have the capacity to absorb a significant amount of capital.

6. Risk Factors: A Deeper Dive Beyond Asset Classes

While the asset class approach is a powerful tool, some investors now look at portfolio risk through an even more granular lens: risk factors. The idea is that the returns of any asset class are really driven by a handful of underlying, fundamental risk factors. Instead of just thinking about "stocks" and "bonds," a factor-based approach thinks about exposures to things like economic growth, inflation, value, size, momentum, and quality.

For example, both value stocks and high-yield bonds might provide exposure to a "credit risk" factor. A traditional asset allocation might see them as distinct, but a factor approach recognizes their common underlying driver. This view helps explain why different asset classes sometimes move together unexpectedly. They are exposed to the same underlying factors.

This approach doesn't necessarily replace the traditional asset class model, but it certainly complements it. By analyzing a portfolio through a factor lens, an investor can get a much clearer understanding of what is truly driving their returns and where their risks are concentrated. For instance, a portfolio might look well-diversified across asset classes, but a factor analysis could reveal that it is heavily dependent on a single factor, like economic growth. This allows for a more precise and robust form of diversification, building a portfolio that is resilient to a wider range of economic scenarios.

7. Recommending and Justifying an Asset Allocation

Creating the right asset allocation for an individual is a deeply personal process. It involves a careful blend of art and science, culminating in a strategy that is tailored to an investor's unique circumstances. The process begins with understanding the investor's objectives and constraints.

The objectives are the "why" of investing. This includes the return objective (what level of return is needed?) and the risk tolerance (how much volatility can the investor emotionally and financially handle?). A young person with a long time horizon can typically afford to take on more risk for higher potential returns, while a retiree will prioritize capital preservation.

The constraints are the "rules" that the portfolio must operate within. These can include liquidity needs (is cash needed in the short term?), the time horizon (when will the money be needed?), tax considerations (is the account taxable or tax-deferred?), and any unique circumstances, such as legal issues or a desire for socially responsible investments.

Let's imagine a 35-year-old investor saving for retirement in 30 years. Her objective is long-term growth. Her risk tolerance is high, and her time horizon is long. She has no immediate liquidity needs. A justified asset allocation for her might be aggressive, for example, 80% in equities (diversified across U.S., international, and emerging markets) and 20% in bonds. The justification is that her long time horizon allows her to weather the short-term volatility of stocks to capture their higher long-term growth potential. The bond allocation provides a small cushion and a source of diversification. This allocation directly aligns with her ability and willingness to take risks to achieve her long-term goals.

8. The Global Market Portfolio: A Neutral Starting Point

When deciding on a strategic asset allocation, where do you start? One powerful concept is the use of the global market portfolio as a baseline. In theory, the global market portfolio includes every single investable asset in the world, weighted by its market value. It would contain every stock, every bond, every piece of real estate, and so on.

Of course, creating the true global market portfolio is impossible in practice. However, it serves as an incredibly useful theoretical benchmark. It represents the ultimate level of diversification. It is the one portfolio held by all investors collectively. As such, it is considered the most neutral or passive portfolio an investor can hold. The returns of this portfolio represent the return that the average investor earns.

For an asset allocation strategist, the global market portfolio provides a disciplined and unbiased starting point. Rather than starting with a blank slate, an analyst can begin with the global market weights and then decide where to deviate based on their specific views or the client's needs. For example, if an analyst believes that emerging markets will outperform, they might recommend an overweight position relative to their weight in the global market portfolio. Any deviation from this baseline must be justified by a belief that it will lead to superior risk-adjusted returns. This approach helps to avoid common behavioral biases, like home-country bias, where investors disproportionately invest in their own country's market.

9. Strategic Implementation: Passive vs. Active Choices and Vehicles

Once the strategic asset allocation is set, the next question is how to implement it. This involves making critical choices, primarily between passive and active management, and selecting the right investment vehicles to gain the desired exposures.

Passive management involves tracking a market index as closely as possible. The goal isn't to beat the market, but to capture the market's return at a very low cost. The argument for passive investing is strong, as a large body of evidence shows that the majority of active managers fail to outperform their benchmarks after fees over the long run.

Active management, on the other hand, is all about trying to beat the market. This involves skilled portfolio managers making specific bets on securities they believe are undervalued or poised for growth. While the potential for outperformance is the main draw, it comes with higher fees and the risk that the manager will underperform the market instead.

The choice between passive and active isn't always all or nothing. Many investors use a core-satellite approach, where the "core" of their portfolio is passively managed in low-cost index funds, while they use actively managed "satellite" positions to seek outperformance in specific areas.

The final piece of the puzzle is selecting the investment vehicles. This can include mutual funds, which are professionally managed pools of assets; exchange-traded funds (ETFs), which trade like stocks and typically offer low costs and tax efficiency; and for very wealthy investors, separately managed accounts, which offer a high degree of customization. The choice depends on factors like cost, tax efficiency, liquidity, and the level of transparency desired.

10. The Strategy of Rebalancing: Staying on Course

An asset allocation strategy is not a "set it and forget it" plan. Over time, as different asset classes perform differently, the portfolio's original weights will drift. For example, if stocks have a great year and bonds are flat, the portfolio will naturally become overweight in stocks and underweight in bonds. This might mean the portfolio is now taking on more risk than was originally intended.

This is where rebalancing comes in. Rebalancing is the process of periodically buying or selling assets in a portfolio to restore its original target asset allocation. It's a disciplined way to manage risk. In essence, it forces you to sell some of the assets that have performed well (sell high) and buy more of the assets that have underperformed (buy low).

There are two main strategic approaches to rebalancing. The first is calendar rebalancing, where the portfolio is reset to its target weights on a regular schedule, such as quarterly or annually. This is simple and easy to implement. The second approach is tolerance-based rebalancing. Here, the portfolio is rebalanced only when the weight of an asset class drifts beyond a predetermined tolerance band, for example, more than 5% away from its target. This method can be more efficient, as it avoids unnecessary trading when market movements are small. The key consideration in any rebalancing strategy is the trade-off between the benefit of risk control and the costs of trading, such as commissions and taxes.

Principles of Asset Allocation

Asset allocation is the cornerstone of successful investing. It's not about picking the winning stock; it's about creating a thoughtful mix of different investments that aligns with your goals and comfort with risk. Think of it as building a team, where each player (or asset class) has a specific role to play in achieving the final victory. This guide breaks down the core principles that drive these critical decisions.

Describing and Evaluating Mean-Variance Optimization

At its heart, mean-variance optimization (MVO) is a powerful mathematical tool designed to find the sweet spot in investing. It helps us build a portfolio that offers the highest possible expected return (the "mean") for whatever level of risk we're willing to stomach (the "variance"). Imagine a graph where you plot hundreds of possible portfolios. MVO identifies a curved line of the best possible options, known as the "efficient frontier." Any portfolio on this line is considered optimal because you can't get a higher return without also taking on more risk. It's a beautifully logical approach.

However, MVO has its limitations. Its biggest challenge is that it relies on inputs—expected returns, risks, and correlations—that are based on historical data. And as we all know, the past is not a perfect predictor of the future. The model is highly sensitive, meaning a tiny change in an input can drastically alter the recommended portfolio. It's a fantastic starting point for a conversation, but it's not a crystal ball.

Recommending an Asset Allocation Using Mean-Variance Optimization

Using MVO to recommend an allocation is a collaborative process. First, we run the numbers to generate that efficient frontier, which visually shows the client the trade-off between risk and return. Then, the conversation begins. We might ask, "Here is a portfolio with a 7% expected return but could see a 15% drop in a bad year. And here is one with a 5% expected return that likely won't drop more than 8%. Which one lets you sleep at night?" The final recommendation is the specific mix of assets on the frontier that best matches the investor's unique tolerance for risk.

Interpreting an Allocation in Relation to an Investor's Economic Balance Sheet

An investor's economic balance sheet is a much broader, more holistic view of their financial world. It includes not just traditional financial assets like stocks and bonds, but also less obvious ones like human capital (your future lifetime earnings) and real estate. Thinking this way completely changes the game. For example, a young surgeon with decades of stable, high earnings ahead has massive, bond-like human capital. This means she can afford to take much more risk in her investment portfolio. In contrast, a retired factory worker has very little human capital left and relies entirely on their financial assets, suggesting a much more conservative allocation is needed.

Recommending an Asset Allocation Based on the Global Market Portfolio

The global market portfolio is the ultimate benchmark for diversification. In theory, it includes a small piece of every single investable asset in the world—every stock, bond, and piece of real estate, all weighted by their total market value. The logic is that this represents the collective wisdom of all investors and is, therefore, the most efficient portfolio possible. A practical recommendation based on this concept would be to start with a portfolio of low-cost index funds that mimic the global stock and bond markets. From there, you can tilt the allocation slightly to reflect an investor's personal views, risk tolerance, or unique circumstances.

Using Monte Carlo Simulation and Scenario Analysis

If MVO gives us a single expected outcome, Monte Carlo simulation gives us thousands of them. It's a powerful computer-based method that stress-tests a portfolio by running it through a huge number of potential future market conditions. This doesn't tell you what will happen, but it gives you a realistic range of what could happen. You can see the probability of reaching your retirement goal, or the potential severity of the worst-case scenario. Scenario analysis is similar but more targeted. It asks specific "what-if" questions, like "What happens to my portfolio if we see a repeat of the 2008 financial crisis?" Both tools help test if an allocation is truly robust.

Asset Class Liquidity Considerations

Liquidity is simply how quickly you can convert an asset into cash without losing a significant amount of its value. Publicly traded stocks are highly liquid; you can sell them in seconds. On the other hand, assets like private equity, venture capital, or a commercial building are highly illiquid—it could take months or even years to sell them. When building a portfolio, you absolutely must consider liquidity needs. If an investor needs to fund a large down payment on a house in six months, that money should be in liquid, stable assets, not tied up in something that can't be sold easily.

Absolute and Relative Risk Budgets

A risk budget is a clear framework for deciding how much risk to take and where to take it. There are two main types. An absolute risk budget sets a hard ceiling on potential losses, often measured in dollar amounts or percentages. For example, a pension fund might say, "We cannot tolerate a loss of more than 10% of the portfolio's value in any given year." A relative risk budget, common among fund managers, measures risk against a benchmark. A manager might be told, "Your goal is to beat the S&P 500, but your tracking error cannot exceed 3%," meaning their performance can't deviate too far from the index.

Incorporating Client Risk Preferences

This is where the art of financial advice meets the science. An investor's true risk tolerance is a complex mix of their financial ability to take risks and their emotional willingness to do so. A questionnaire can be a good starting point, but the best insights come from deep conversations. We need to understand their past experiences with money, their anxieties, and their aspirations. The goal is to build a portfolio that is not only mathematically sound but also behaviorally durable—one the investor can stick with through the market's inevitable ups and downs without panicking.

Using Investment Factors

Factor investing takes us a layer deeper than traditional asset allocation. Instead of just thinking about stocks versus bonds, it looks at the underlying characteristics, or "factors," that drive returns across different asset classes. Well-researched factors include Value (buying assets that are cheap relative to their fundamentals), Momentum (investing in assets with strong recent performance), Quality (focusing on financially healthy companies), and Size (small-cap stocks historically outperforming large-caps). By consciously tilting a portfolio toward these factors, an investor can potentially enhance returns and improve diversification.

Characteristics of Liabilities Relevant to Asset Allocation

For many investors, especially institutions like pension funds and insurance companies, the portfolio exists for one reason: to meet a future set of financial obligations, or liabilities. To do this properly, you have to deeply understand those liabilities. Are they fixed or do they grow with inflation? When are they due (what's the timing)? How certain is the amount? A university endowment has a perpetual time horizon, while a person saving for retirement has a very specific date in mind. The nature of the liability is the single most important driver of the investment strategy.

Approaches to Liability-Relative Asset Allocation

Liability-relative investing, often called Liability-Driven Investing (LDI), flips the traditional script. Instead of focusing on maximizing returns relative to a market benchmark, the primary goal is to ensure the assets are sufficient to cover liabilities. A common approach is to divide the portfolio into two parts. One is a "hedging portfolio" (or matching portfolio), typically composed of high-quality bonds, designed to move in value with the liabilities and reduce risk. The second is a "growth portfolio," which takes on more risk with assets like stocks and real estate, with the goal of generating returns to reduce any funding shortfall.

Recommending and Justifying a Liability-Relative Asset Allocation

Let's say we're advising a pension plan that is currently underfunded. A sound recommendation would be to allocate a significant portion of its assets to a bond portfolio with a duration that closely matches the duration of its pension payouts. This locks in the plan's ability to meet a large chunk of its future obligations. We would justify this by explaining that it dramatically reduces the risk that rising interest rates will harm their funding status. The remaining assets could then be invested in a diversified pool of growth assets to close the funding gap over time. The key is to secure the promise first, then seek growth.

Recommending and Justifying a Goals-Based Approach

Goals-based allocation is an incredibly intuitive and powerful way to structure a portfolio. Instead of viewing all their money in one big pot, an investor creates separate "buckets" for each of their major life goals. They might have a "Retirement" bucket (long-term, high allocation to stocks), a "Kids' College" bucket (medium-term, balanced mix), and a "Home Down Payment" bucket (short-term, very conservative). We can justify this approach because it directly connects their investments to their life. This mental accounting makes it easier for them to understand the risks being taken and to stay the course when one part of the market is struggling.

Describing and Evaluating Heuristic Approaches

Heuristics are essentially rules of thumb. They are simple, practical shortcuts for making complex decisions. In asset allocation, a famous heuristic is the "100 minus your age" rule, which suggests the percentage of your portfolio that should be in stocks. Another is the "1/N" strategy, where you simply divide your money equally among N different asset classes. While these approaches lack the mathematical rigor of MVO, they are incredibly easy to understand and implement. Their biggest benefit is that they provide a disciplined framework that can prevent investors from making purely emotional, often disastrous, decisions.

Discussing Factors Affecting Rebalancing Policy

Rebalancing is the discipline of periodically buying or selling assets to maintain your original target asset allocation. For instance, if your 60/40 stock/bond portfolio drifts to 70/30 after a great year for stocks, you would sell some stocks and buy some bonds to get back to 60/40. The key factors that affect how you do this are transaction costs (rebalancing too often can be expensive), taxes (selling winners can trigger capital gains), and how much drift you're willing to tolerate. A common policy is to rebalance on a set schedule, like annually, or whenever an asset class moves beyond a predetermined band, like 5% from its target.

Asset Allocation with Real-World Constraints

Navigating the Real World: Constraints on Asset Allocation

Asset allocation isn't just about picking stocks and bonds; it's a deeply personal process shaped by the realities of an investor's life. Think of it like tailoring a suit. A generic, off-the-rack portfolio simply won't do. It needs to be custom-fitted to your specific circumstances, and that's where constraints come in.

First, let's talk about asset size. The amount of money you have to invest dramatically changes the game. A multi-million dollar portfolio has access to a world of opportunities, like private equity, hedge funds, or direct real estate investments, that are simply out of reach for someone starting with a few thousand dollars. These alternative investments often have high minimum buy-ins and can offer diversification benefits not found in public markets. For the smaller investor, the focus is often on achieving broad diversification through more accessible means, like low-cost exchange-traded funds (ETFs) and mutual funds. The sheer scale of a large portfolio also means that even small percentage allocations can represent significant dollar amounts, requiring a more granular approach to management.

Next up is liquidity needs. Life is unpredictable. An emergency fund isn't an investment; it's a necessity. Liquidity refers to how quickly you can convert an asset into cash without losing a significant chunk of its value. If you're saving for a down payment on a house in the next year, putting that money into a volatile growth stock is a recipe for disaster. You need that cash to be safe and accessible. This means a portion of your portfolio must be in highly liquid, low-risk assets like high-yield savings accounts, money market funds, or short-term government bonds. The higher your potential need for immediate cash, the larger this "safe" allocation needs to be, which naturally constrains how much you can allocate to riskier, long-term growth assets.

The time horizon is perhaps the most powerful constraint of all. It's the length of time you have until you need to start drawing money from your investments. A 25-year-old saving for retirement has decades to ride out the market's inevitable ups and downs. They can afford to take on more risk by allocating a larger portion of their portfolio to stocks, knowing that over the long run, stocks have historically provided the highest returns. Time is their greatest ally, allowing them to recover from market downturns. In stark contrast, someone who is five years from retirement has a much shorter runway. A major market crash could devastate their nest egg with little time to recoup the losses. Their allocation must be more conservative, with a greater emphasis on capital preservation through a higher allocation to bonds and other stable assets.

Finally, we have regulatory and other considerations. This is a broad category that can include anything from legal restrictions to personal values. For instance, a corporate insider might be legally restricted from trading their company's stock during certain periods. A university endowment fund might have specific rules in its charter about the types of investments it can make. On a more personal level, an investor might choose to engage in socially responsible investing (SRI) or environmental, social, and governance (ESG) investing. This means they will actively avoid allocating capital to companies involved in industries they find objectionable, such as tobacco, firearms, or fossil fuels, regardless of their potential for high returns. These self-imposed or legally-mandated rules act as firm guardrails, directly shaping the final asset allocation.

The Taxman Cometh: How Taxes Shape Your Portfolio

Taxes are one of life's certainties, and they have a profound impact on investment returns. A savvy investor doesn't just think about what they earn; they think about what they keep. Ignoring tax implications is like running a race with weights on your ankles—it needlessly slows you down.

The first major consideration is asset location. This isn't about where you live; it's about which type of account you use to hold different assets. You generally want to place your least tax-efficient assets in tax-advantaged accounts, like a 401(k) or an IRA. These are assets that generate a lot of taxable income each year, such as corporate bonds that pay regular interest or actively managed mutual funds that have high turnover and generate frequent capital gains. By holding them in a tax-deferred or tax-free account, you shield that income from annual taxation, allowing it to compound more effectively. Conversely, you would place your most tax-efficient assets, like broad-market index funds or individual stocks you plan to hold for the long term, in a regular taxable brokerage account. Since these assets generate fewer taxable events, the tax drag is less severe.

When it comes to rebalancing, taxes add another layer of complexity. Rebalancing is the crucial process of selling assets that have grown to be overweight in your portfolio and buying assets that have become underweight, in order to return to your target allocation. The problem is that selling winning investments in a taxable account triggers a capital gains tax. To manage this, investors can employ several strategies. One is to rebalance using new contributions. Instead of selling winners, you simply direct new money into the underperforming asset classes until the portfolio is back in balance. Another strategy is tax-loss harvesting. This involves selling an investment that has lost value to realize a capital loss. That loss can then be used to offset capital gains from your winning investments, reducing your overall tax bill. You can then immediately buy a similar, but not "substantially identical," investment to maintain your desired market exposure, cleverly avoiding the IRS's "wash sale" rule. Careful planning around rebalancing can save a significant amount of money over an investor's lifetime.

Finally, the type of investment income itself is taxed differently. Long-term capital gains (from assets held for more than a year) and qualified dividends are typically taxed at a lower rate than ordinary income, which includes short-term capital gains and bond interest. This creates a clear incentive to be a long-term investor. It also influences asset selection. For an investor in a high tax bracket, a municipal bond, whose interest is often exempt from federal (and sometimes state) taxes, might offer a better after-tax return than a corporate bond with a higher pre-tax yield. Understanding these nuances allows an investor and their advisor to build a portfolio that is not just effective, but also tax-smart.

Adapting to Life's Changes: Revising Your Asset Allocation

An asset allocation strategy is not a "set it and forget it" plan. It's a living document that must evolve as your life circumstances, goals, and constraints change. Sticking to an outdated allocation is like trying to navigate a new city with an old map—you're unlikely to end up where you want to go. The ability to recommend and justify revisions is a hallmark of sound financial planning.

Let's consider a common scenario: a change in investment objectives. Imagine a young couple in their early 30s. Their initial objective was aggressive growth for retirement, which is 30+ years away. Their portfolio was heavily weighted towards equities, perhaps 85% stocks and 15% bonds. Then, they decide they want to buy a house in the next five years. Their investment objective has now shifted. They still have the long-term goal of retirement, but now a significant, medium-term goal has been introduced. Keeping the down payment savings in a high-risk stock portfolio would be irresponsible. A crash could postpone their homeownership dream indefinitely.

The justified revision would be to carve out a separate "bucket" for the down payment. This money should be moved to a much more conservative allocation, perhaps a mix of short-term bond funds, CDs, and a high-yield savings account. This protects the principal from market volatility. Consequently, their overall asset allocation will become more conservative. While their retirement bucket might remain at 85/15, the new, safer bucket for the house fund will pull the total portfolio's stock allocation down. The justification is clear: the introduction of a short-term goal with a low tolerance for risk necessitates a corresponding reduction in portfolio risk to ensure that goal can be met.

Now, let's look at a change in constraints. Suppose a 50-year-old investor receives a large inheritance. This drastically changes their asset size constraint. Their previous portfolio was well-managed but limited to publicly traded stocks and bonds. With this new, significant capital, their investment universe expands. A recommendation to revise the asset allocation would be to incorporate alternative investments. The justification is diversification. The investor could now allocate a small percentage, say 5-10%, to assets like private real estate or a venture capital fund. These assets have a low correlation to the public stock and bond markets, meaning they don't always move in the same direction. During a stock market downturn, these alternatives can help stabilize the overall portfolio's value. The revision is justified by the opportunity to reduce overall portfolio volatility and potentially enhance long-term returns, an opportunity that was not available before the inheritance changed their financial picture. In every case, the key is to clearly link the recommended change back to the specific shift in the investor's objectives or constraints, ensuring the portfolio remains a true reflection of their financial life.

Riding the Waves: The Use of Short-Term Shifts

While strategic asset allocation is the bedrock of a long-term investment plan, setting your target percentages for stocks, bonds, and other assets, there's a related concept known as tactical asset allocation. This involves making short-term shifts away from your strategic targets to capitalize on perceived market opportunities or to sidestep potential risks. It's a more active approach, like a sailor adjusting the sails to catch a favorable wind, rather than just pointing the ship in the right direction and hoping for the best.

The core idea is to be flexible. A purely strategic investor might stick to a 60% stock, 40% bond mix through thick and thin, rebalancing back to those numbers periodically. A tactical investor, however, might believe that stocks are becoming overvalued after a long bull run and that bonds look relatively cheap. In this case, they might temporarily shift their allocation to, say, 55% stocks and 45% bonds. They aren't abandoning their long-term strategy; they are simply making a temporary, or "tactical," deviation with the goal of enhancing returns or reducing risk. If their thesis plays out and stocks correct, they have cushioned the blow. If stocks continue to rise, they still participate, just to a lesser degree.

These shifts are not wild guesses; they are typically based on a systematic evaluation of market indicators. Analysts might look at economic data like GDP growth, inflation rates, and employment figures. They also use valuation metrics, such as the price-to-earnings (P/E) ratio for the stock market, to gauge whether an asset class appears expensive or inexpensive relative to its historical average. For example, if the P/E ratio of the S&P 500 creeps into its highest historical decile, a tactical manager might see this as a signal of froth and reduce their equity exposure. Conversely, if investor sentiment is extremely pessimistic and market valuations are low, they might see a buying opportunity and tactically increase their allocation to stocks.

However, this strategy is not without its challenges and risks. The biggest risk is simply being wrong. Market timing is notoriously difficult, even for seasoned professionals. Shifting out of stocks just before a final, powerful surge in a bull market can lead to significant underperformance and regret. Furthermore, frequent trading can rack up transaction costs and, in a taxable account, generate higher taxes, both of which eat into returns. For these reasons, tactical shifts are usually done within a predefined range. For example, the long-term strategic target for stocks might be 60%, but the investment policy allows for a tactical band of 50% to 70%. This provides the flexibility to be active without allowing a single bad call to completely derail the long-term plan. It's a tool for optimization, not a replacement for a solid, strategic foundation.

Mind Over Money: Overcoming Behavioral Biases

Investing should be a rational process, but we are not robots. We are humans, driven by a complex mix of logic and emotion. This is where behavioral finance comes in, studying the psychological biases that cause investors to make irrational decisions, often to their own detriment. Identifying these biases is the first step toward building a more disciplined and successful asset allocation strategy.

One of the most powerful biases is loss aversion. Psychologically, the pain of a loss is felt about twice as strongly as the pleasure of an equivalent gain. This can lead to irrational behavior. For example, an investor might hold on to a losing stock for far too long, hoping it will "come back" to what they paid for it, even when all fundamental signs point to further declines. They are so averse to crystallizing the loss that they end up taking an even bigger one. To overcome this, one method is to ask a simple question: "If I had the cash today, would I buy this investment?" If the answer is no, it's time to sell, regardless of its history. Setting a pre-determined stop-loss order, which automatically sells a security if it drops to a certain price, can also take the emotional decision out of the investor's hands.

Another common pitfall is recency bias, which is the tendency to overweight recent events when making decisions. After a long bull market, investors can become complacent and overconfident, piling into stocks at the top because they extrapolate recent high returns indefinitely into the future. This leads to an asset allocation that is far too risky. Conversely, after a scary market crash, investors become overly fearful, selling their stocks at the bottom and vowing never to return. To combat this, it's crucial to have a written Investment Policy Statement (IPS). This document outlines your long-term goals, risk tolerance, and strategic asset allocation. During periods of market euphoria or panic, you can refer back to your IPS. It serves as a rational anchor, reminding you of the plan you made when you were thinking clearly and calmly.

Finally, there's herd mentality, the natural human instinct to follow the crowd. When everyone is buzzing about a hot tech stock or a new cryptocurrency, the fear of missing out (FOMO) can be overwhelming. Investors abandon their carefully constructed, diversified portfolios to chase the latest fad, often buying in at the peak of the hype cycle. The best defense against this is discipline and a commitment to your long-term plan. Automating your investments, where money is regularly transferred and invested according to your target allocation, can be incredibly effective. It forces you to be disciplined, to buy systematically whether the market is up or down. Working with a financial advisor can also provide a crucial "behavioral coach," an objective voice of reason to talk you down from the ledge when fear or greed threatens to derail your strategy. Ultimately, overcoming these biases is about creating a system that separates your emotions from your investment decisions.

Chapter 2: Portfolio Construction

Overview of Equity Portfolio Management

Equity portfolio management is a dynamic and multifaceted discipline that sits at the heart of modern investing. It's the art and science of selecting, managing, and overseeing a collection of stocks, or equities, to meet specific investment goals. For many investors, equities are the primary engine for wealth creation, but harnessing their potential requires a deep understanding of their role, the costs involved, and the strategic decisions that drive performance. This overview explores the foundational concepts of managing an equity portfolio, from its basic purpose to the nuanced considerations of benchmarking and shareholder advocacy.

The Role of Equities in an Overall Portfolio

Equities, or stocks, represent ownership in a company. They are a cornerstone of most investment portfolios for one primary reason: their potential for significant capital appreciation. Over the long term, equities have historically delivered higher returns than other major asset classes like bonds or cash. This growth potential is crucial for investors looking to outpace inflation and build substantial wealth over time. When you own a stock, you have a claim on the company's future earnings and assets, which can lead to a rising stock price as the company succeeds.

Beyond just growth, equities also offer a source of income through dividends. Many established companies share a portion of their profits with shareholders, providing a regular cash flow that can be either reinvested to purchase more shares or used as income. This combination of growth and income makes equities incredibly versatile.

Furthermore, equities play a vital role in portfolio diversification. While they are considered riskier than bonds, including them in a mixed-asset portfolio can actually help manage overall risk. Different asset classes often perform differently under various economic conditions. For instance, in a strong economy, equities might soar while certain bonds may not. By holding a mix, the poor performance of one asset can be offset by the strong performance of another, creating a more stable and resilient portfolio that is better equipped to handle market volatility.

Segmenting an Equity Manager's Investment Universe

The world of stocks is vast, and no portfolio manager can analyze every single company. To make the task manageable and to build a focused strategy, managers segment the equity "universe" into smaller, more coherent categories. This process allows them to develop expertise in specific areas and align their portfolios with particular investment objectives.

One of the most common ways to segment the market is by company size, or market capitalization. This gives us categories like large-cap (large, well-established companies), mid-cap (medium-sized companies with room for growth), and small-cap (smaller, often younger companies with high growth potential but also higher risk). Each segment has its own risk and return characteristics.

Another key method is by investment style. This divides stocks into "growth" and "value" categories. Growth stocks are shares in companies expected to grow faster than the overall market, often reinvesting their profits to expand rather than paying dividends. Think of technology or innovative healthcare companies. Value stocks, on the other hand, are stocks that appear to be trading for less than their intrinsic worth. A manager might look for solid, established companies that are temporarily out of favor with the market.

Additionally, equities can be segmented by geography (e.g., U.S. stocks, international developed markets, or emerging markets) and by economic sector (e.g., technology, healthcare, financials, energy, or consumer staples). By combining these different segmentation methods, a portfolio manager can precisely define their investment universe, such as "U.S. large-cap value stocks" or "emerging markets technology stocks," creating a clear and disciplined approach to stock selection.

Income and Costs in an Equity Portfolio

Owning and managing an equity portfolio involves both sources of income and various costs, all of which directly impact the final return an investor receives. The primary sources of income are straightforward. Capital gains occur when a stock is sold for a higher price than it was purchased for. Dividends represent a share of the company's profits distributed to shareholders, providing a regular income stream.

On the other side of the ledger are the costs, which can sometimes be less obvious. Management fees are charged by professional portfolio managers or mutual funds for their expertise and services, typically calculated as a percentage of the assets under management. Trading costs, or brokerage commissions, are fees paid every time a stock is bought or sold. Frequent trading can cause these costs to add up quickly, eating into profits.

Another significant but often overlooked cost is the bid-ask spread. This is the small difference between the highest price a buyer is willing to pay for a stock (the bid) and the lowest price a seller is willing to accept (the ask). This spread is effectively a hidden transaction cost. Finally, taxes are a major consideration. Capital gains and dividend income are often subject to taxes, which can significantly reduce the net return. The way a portfolio is managed—for instance, how frequently stocks are sold—can have a substantial impact on the tax bill. A successful manager must not only generate returns but also diligently control these costs to maximize performance.

Shareholder Engagement and its Benefits

Shareholder engagement, sometimes called shareholder activism or advocacy, is the process through which investors use their ownership stake to influence a company's behavior and decision-making. This goes beyond simply buying and selling stocks. An engaged equity manager actively communicates with a company's management or board of directors to push for changes that they believe will unlock more value for shareholders in the long run.

The potential benefits are substantial. One of the primary goals of engagement is to improve corporate governance. This could involve advocating for a more independent board of directors, better executive compensation structures that align with long-term performance, or greater transparency in financial reporting. Stronger governance often leads to better-managed, more resilient, and more profitable companies.

Engagement is also a powerful tool for promoting environmental, social, and governance (ESG) principles. A manager might pressure a company to reduce its carbon footprint, improve its labor practices, or enhance the diversity of its workforce. These changes can not only lead to a more sustainable and ethical company but can also reduce long-term risks and open up new market opportunities, ultimately benefiting the stock price. By acting as a responsible steward of capital, an equity manager can do more than just pick winning stocks; they can actively help create them, fostering long-term value that benefits the company, its shareholders, and society at large.

Rationales for Equity Investment Across the Active Management Spectrum

When it comes to managing an equity portfolio, investors can choose from a spectrum of approaches, ranging from purely passive to highly active. Each approach has a distinct rationale and is suited to different beliefs about the market.

At one end of the spectrum is passive management, most commonly executed through index funds or exchange-traded funds (ETFs). The core rationale here is the efficient market hypothesis, which suggests that stock prices already reflect all available information, making it nearly impossible to consistently outperform the market. A passive manager doesn't try to pick winners; instead, they simply aim to replicate the performance of a specific market index, like the S&P 500. The main advantages are very low costs and broad diversification.

At the other end is active management. The rationale for this approach is the belief that markets are not perfectly efficient and that skilled managers can identify mispriced stocks to generate returns that beat the market index (known as "alpha"). Active managers conduct in-depth research, analyze financial statements, and make deliberate decisions about which stocks to buy, hold, or sell. This approach is more expensive due to the research and trading involved, but it offers the potential for superior returns.

Between these two extremes lie various hybrid or "smart beta" strategies. These strategies start with a passive index but then apply specific rules-based tilts. For example, a fund might track the S&P 500 but overweight stocks that have strong value or momentum characteristics. The rationale is to capture some of the benefits of active insights while maintaining lower costs and a more disciplined, systematic approach. The choice along this spectrum ultimately depends on an investor's goals, risk tolerance, and belief in the manager's ability to add value.

Considerations in Choosing a Benchmark for an Equity Portfolio

A benchmark is a standard against which the performance of a portfolio is measured. It serves as a critical reference point, helping to answer the question, "Did my portfolio do well?" Choosing the right benchmark is essential for properly evaluating a manager's skill and ensuring the portfolio is on track to meet its goals. An inappropriate benchmark can be misleading, making a poor manager look good or an excellent manager look average.

The most important consideration is that the benchmark must be appropriate and accurately reflect the portfolio's investment style and strategy. For example, a portfolio of U.S. small-cap growth stocks should not be measured against the S&P 500, which is a large-cap index. A more suitable benchmark would be the Russell 2000 Growth Index. The benchmark should align with the portfolio's market capitalization, style (growth vs. value), and geographic focus.

A good benchmark should also be investable—meaning an investor could, in theory, replicate it by buying the underlying securities. It needs to be measurable, with its value calculated and published on a regular basis. Furthermore, it should be unambiguous, with clearly defined constituent securities. Finally, it should be specified in advance, before the evaluation period begins, to avoid any bias. By selecting a benchmark that truly represents the manager's stated investment universe, investors can gain a clear and accurate picture of the value being added (or not added) by the manager's active decisions.

Overview of Fixed-Income Portfolio Management

Roles and Classification of Fixed-Income Mandates

Fixed-income securities, often simply called bonds, play several vital roles within a well-rounded investment portfolio. Think of them as the steady foundation of a house. Their primary job is often diversification. Because bond prices don't always move in the same direction as stock prices, they can provide a cushion when the stock market is volatile. Another key role is generating regular, predictable income. The coupon payments from bonds create a steady stream of cash flow, which is incredibly valuable for retirees or anyone needing consistent income. Finally, high-quality bonds are excellent for capital preservation. They are generally safer than stocks, helping to protect an investor's initial capital from significant loss.

Portfolio mandates for fixed income are classified in various ways. They can be categorized by risk, such as investment-grade versus high-yield ("junk") bonds. They might also be grouped by maturity—short-term, intermediate-term, or long-term. Other classifications include the type of issuer (government, corporate, or municipal) or the management style, which can be either active (trying to beat the market) or passive (tracking an index).

Measures of Risk, Return, and Correlation

To manage a bond portfolio effectively, we need ways to measure its performance and risk. For returns, the most common measure is Yield-to-Maturity (YTM), which tells you the total return you can expect if you hold a bond until it matures. A more holistic view is the total return, which includes both the coupon income and any change in the bond's market price.

On the risk side, the most important concept is duration. Duration measures how sensitive a bond's price is to changes in interest rates. A higher duration means a small change in rates will cause a larger change in the bond's price, making it riskier. Another key risk is credit risk—the chance that the issuer won't be able to make its payments. This is assessed using credit ratings from agencies like S&P and Moody's.

A defining characteristic of fixed income is its correlation to other assets. High-quality bonds typically have a low or even negative correlation with stocks. This is what makes them such powerful diversifiers; they often zig when stocks zag.

Bond Market Liquidity

Liquidity refers to how easily an asset can be bought or sold at a fair price. In the bond market, liquidity varies dramatically. The most liquid securities are newly issued government bonds, like U.S. Treasuries. The market for these is enormous and transactions are easy. Moving down the scale, older government bonds and bonds from large, well-known corporations are also quite liquid, though less so.

However, many parts of the bond market are much less liquid. This includes municipal bonds, high-yield corporate bonds, and certain mortgage-backed securities. These often trade in over-the-counter markets where finding a buyer or seller can take time and impact the price. This lack of liquidity has a real effect on portfolio management. Managers demand a higher yield (a "liquidity premium") for holding these less-traded bonds. They must also carefully manage the portfolio to ensure they can meet any cash needs without being forced to sell illiquid assets at a steep discount, especially during times of market stress.

A Model for Fixed-Income Returns

Understanding what drives bond returns helps managers make better decisions. We can break down the total return of a bond into a few key parts. The most straightforward component is the yield income, which is simply the return you get from the bond's coupon payments. It's the most predictable piece of the puzzle.

Another part is the rolldown return. If the yield curve is upward-sloping (meaning longer-term bonds have higher yields), a bond's price will naturally increase as it gets closer to maturity and "rolls down" the curve to a lower yield. The biggest and most volatile component, however, comes from changes in price due to shifts in interest rates and credit spreads. This is where duration really matters. If rates go up or credit fears cause spreads to widen, bond prices will fall. For international bonds, you also have to add currency gains or losses to the model.

Leverage in Fixed-Income Portfolios

Leverage means using borrowed money to invest, with the goal of amplifying returns. In fixed-income, a manager might borrow at a low short-term rate to invest in bonds that offer a higher yield, capturing the spread. The most common way to do this is through repurchase agreements, or "repos." This involves selling a bond to a lender with an agreement to buy it back shortly after at a slightly higher price. Other methods include using futures contracts or derivatives like interest rate swaps to gain exposure without buying the bonds outright.

While leverage can boost returns, it also introduces significant risks. It magnifies losses just as much as it magnifies gains. A small negative move in the market can lead to a very large loss. The biggest danger is funding risk. If the short-term lending market freezes up, as it did in 2008, a manager might not be able to renew their loans. This could force them to sell assets at deeply depressed prices to pay back the debt, creating a devastating downward spiral.

Managing for Taxable vs. Tax-Exempt Investors

The right fixed-income strategy depends heavily on the investor's tax situation. A taxable investor, like an individual, cares about their after-tax return. For them, municipal bonds can be very attractive because their interest income is often free from federal, state, and local taxes. A lower-yielding municipal bond can end up providing a better after-tax return than a higher-yielding corporate bond. Taxable investors also have to consider capital gains taxes and may use strategies like tax-loss harvesting to improve their tax efficiency.

In contrast, a tax-exempt investor, such as a pension fund or an endowment, is focused on pre-tax return. Since they don't pay taxes on investment income, they simply want the highest yield for a given level of risk. For them, a taxable corporate bond is almost always a better choice than a municipal bond because it offers a higher starting yield. The tax-exempt status of the municipal bond provides them no extra benefit, so they ignore it and focus solely on maximizing pre-tax total return.

Liability-Driven Investing (LDI)

Liability-Driven Investing, or LDI, is a strategy that focuses on managing assets to ensure that future obligations can be met. This approach is most common among pension funds, which have predictable pension payments to make to retirees, and insurance companies, which have future claims to pay.

The goal of LDI is not to beat a market index, but to make sure the money is there when it's needed. The process starts by modeling out the future liabilities to understand their size, timing, and sensitivity to interest rates. Then, a portfolio of bonds is constructed whose cash flows and duration closely match those of the liabilities. By aligning the assets with the liabilities, the plan becomes "immunized" against interest rate risk. If rates fall, the value of the liabilities will go up, but so will the value of the bond portfolio, preventing a funding gap from opening up.

The Strategy of Cash Flow Matching

Cash flow matching is the most direct and conservative form of liability-driven investing. It involves building a dedicated portfolio where the coupon and principal payments from the bonds are timed to exactly match the schedule of upcoming liability payments. For example, if a pension plan needs to pay out $5 million in ten years, the manager could buy a high-quality zero-coupon bond that matures in exactly ten years with a face value of $5 million.

The main benefit of this strategy is that it nearly eliminates interest rate risk. You know with near certainty that the specific cash amounts will be available on the exact dates they are needed. However, this precision comes with limitations. It can be a very rigid and expensive strategy. Finding bonds that perfectly match every single liability can be difficult and may force the manager to accept lower yields. Furthermore, the strategy is not flexible if the underlying liabilities happen to change unexpectedly.

The Laddered Bond Portfolio

A laddered portfolio is a straightforward and popular strategy for managing bonds. The construction is simple: you divide your investment capital into equal portions and invest each portion in bonds with staggered maturity dates. For instance, with $100,000, you might build a five-year ladder by putting $20,000 each into bonds maturing in one, two, three, four, and five years. As each bond matures, you reinvest the proceeds into a new five-year bond, maintaining the ladder structure over time.

This approach offers several key benefits. It helps reduce reinvestment risk by preventing you from having to reinvest your entire portfolio at a single point in time when interest rates might be low. It also provides a steady stream of liquidity, as one "rung" of the ladder is always maturing. The main limitation is that it's a passive strategy that may underperform in certain market conditions. Its risk-return profile is moderate; it avoids extremes by averaging out yields across the curve

Asset Allocation to Alternative Investments

The Roles of Alternative Investments in a Portfolio

Think of a traditional portfolio of stocks and bonds as a well-balanced meal. It has its proteins and its carbohydrates. Alternative investments are the spices, the unique ingredients that can elevate the entire dish. Their primary role is diversification. Because alternatives like private equity, hedge funds, real estate, or infrastructure often march to the beat of a different drum than public markets, they can smooth out the bumps in your portfolio's journey. When stocks are down, a well-chosen alternative might be holding steady or even rising.

Beyond just being different, they can offer access to unique sources of return. A venture capital fund, for instance, taps into the growth of young, private companies—a world you can't access by simply buying a stock on the New York Stock Exchange. They can also serve as powerful inflation hedges; assets like real estate or commodities often perform well when the cost of living is rising, protecting your purchasing power.

Alternatives vs. Bonds as Risk Mitigators for an Equity Position

Traditionally, when your stocks took a nosedive, your high-quality bonds were the dependable airbag, often rising in value as investors fled to safety. For decades, this negative correlation was the bedrock of portfolio construction. However, the world is changing. In certain economic environments, like periods of high inflation, stocks and bonds can fall together. This is where alternatives can really shine as a different kind of risk mitigator.

While a government bond's main job is to provide stability and a predictable (though often low) income stream, an alternative investment acts as a risk mitigator in a more complex way. For example, a global macro hedge fund might be positioned to profit from the very volatility that is hurting your stocks. A private credit fund might be earning a steady, high yield from loans that are insulated from public market sentiment. So, while bonds are a passive shield, alternatives can be an active, adaptive form of defense for your equity holdings.

Traditional vs. Risk-Based Approaches to Building a Portfolio

The classic, traditional approach to building a portfolio is like using building blocks. You have a "stock" block, a "bond" block, and maybe a "cash" block. You decide on a percentage for each—say, 60% stocks, 40% bonds—based on historical returns and correlations. When you add alternatives, you're just creating a new block, maybe a 5% allocation to "private equity." This method is simple and easy to understand.

A risk-based approach, however, looks under the hood. It doesn't just see a "stock." It sees the underlying risks that drive the stock's return: economic growth risk, inflation risk, interest rate risk, and so on. This approach tries to build a portfolio by balancing these fundamental risk factors, not just the asset classes themselves. Alternative investments fit beautifully into this framework because they offer very specific and unique risk exposures that can be used to fine-tune the portfolio's overall risk profile with surgical precision.

Key Investment Considerations When Allocating to Alternatives

Diving into alternative investments requires a different mindset and a heavier toolkit than buying public stocks. First and foremost is the need for deep due diligence. You aren't just buying a piece of a well-known company; you are often betting on a specific manager or a niche strategy. Understanding their process, their team, and their track record is absolutely critical.

Fees are another major consideration. Alternatives typically have more complex and higher fee structures, often involving both a management fee and a performance fee (like "2 and 20"). You must be confident that the potential returns justify these costs. Furthermore, many of these investments are highly illiquid, meaning your money could be tied up for years. And don't forget about complexity—understanding the valuation methods for a private company or the derivatives strategy of a hedge fund requires a significant investment in education and time.

Suitability: Who Should Be Investing in Alternatives?

Alternative investments are not for everyone. The first gatekeeper is financial suitability. Regulators often restrict these investments to "accredited" or "qualified" investors, meaning individuals with a certain level of income or net worth. This is to ensure that investors can withstand a potential total loss of their investment without it devastating their financial well-being.

But beyond just the numbers, there's a question of investor temperament. Are you patient? You need to be, as returns can take many years to materialize. Can you handle complexity and ambiguity? Valuations might be infrequent and based on estimates, not a daily market price. An investor in alternatives needs a long-term horizon, a high tolerance for illiquidity, and the emotional fortitude to stick with a strategy through market cycles without panicking. A financial advisor plays a crucial role here in determining if a client has both the financial capacity and the psychological makeup for this journey.

Approaches to Allocating Capital to Alternatives

Once you've decided alternatives are a good fit, how do you actually allocate to them? One straightforward approach is the "bucket" method. You might have a "growth" bucket (with stocks and private equity), an "income" bucket (with bonds and private credit), and a "preservation" or "diversifier" bucket (with some hedge funds or real assets). This is an intuitive way to categorize investments by their role in the portfolio.

A more sophisticated method uses quantitative models, like mean-variance optimization, to find the "optimal" allocation that maximizes return for a given level of risk. The challenge here is that data for alternatives is often scarce and less reliable than public market data, making these models tricky to implement. Often, the most practical approach is a blend: starting with a target allocation based on long-term goals and then refining it based on manager selection and the specific opportunities currently available in the market.

The Critical Importance of Liquidity Planning

Liquidity—or the ability to turn your investment into cash quickly—is perhaps the most overlooked and important aspect of investing in alternatives. When you allocate to a private equity or venture capital fund, you are making a commitment. The fund manager will make "capital calls," requiring you to send in your pledged money over several years as they find new investments. You can't just sell your stake on a whim.

This means you must plan meticulously. An investor needs a clear picture of their future cash needs for things like retirement, tuition, or taxes. You have to maintain a sufficient buffer of liquid assets (cash, public stocks, bonds) to meet any unexpected life events without being forced to try and sell an illiquid alternative investment at a fire-sale price. Failing to plan for liquidity can turn a great investment into a personal financial crisis.

Monitoring Your Alternative Investment Program

Monitoring an alternative investment is not like checking a stock quote on your phone. It's an ongoing, active process. You aren't just tracking a price; you are monitoring a business plan. This involves regular communication with the fund manager through quarterly reports, investor calls, and annual meetings.

You need to ask critical questions. Is the manager sticking to the strategy you originally bought into? How are the underlying assets in the portfolio performing? Are they making progress toward their stated goals? It's also vital to monitor your overall program. Are your allocations still in line with your targets? Do you need to plan for new commitments as older funds mature and return capital? Effective monitoring ensures your alternative investments stay on track to fulfill their intended role in your portfolio over the long haul.

An Overview of Private Wealth Management

The Landscape of Individual Wealth: Creation and Global Distribution

Wealth, in its simplest form, is what you own. But when we peel back the layers, it becomes a much richer concept. For individuals, wealth isn't just the money in a bank account; it's a diverse portfolio of assets. We can broadly categorize these into two main types: financial wealth and non-financial wealth. Financial wealth is the most liquid and easily measured. It includes things like cash, stocks, bonds, and mutual funds. These are the assets that can be relatively quickly converted into cash to spend or reinvest.

Then there's non-financial wealth, which often represents a significant portion of an individual's net worth. The most common example is real estate—your home, an investment property, or undeveloped land. This category also includes business equity for entrepreneurs, precious metals like gold, valuable art, and collectibles. More abstractly, but critically important, is human capital. This is the present value of your future earning potential from your skills, knowledge, and labor. For a young professional, their human capital is often their single greatest asset, far outweighing their current financial capital.

Wealth creation is a dynamic process. It primarily stems from savings and investment. When individuals earn more than they spend, they create savings. This surplus can then be invested in assets that have the potential to grow in value or generate income, such as buying stocks that appreciate or rental properties that produce monthly cash flow. Entrepreneurship is another powerful engine of wealth creation, where individuals build businesses that create value, jobs, and ultimately, personal fortune.

The distribution of this created wealth across the globe is famously uneven. A small percentage of the world's population holds a disproportionately large share of its wealth. This concentration is often visualized as a pyramid, with a vast number of people with very little wealth at the base and a tiny, ultra-wealthy elite at the peak. Factors like historical economic development, political stability, educational opportunities, and local market dynamics all contribute to this disparity. Developed regions like North America and Europe have traditionally held the largest shares of global wealth, but emerging economies, particularly in Asia, are rapidly closing the gap, minting new millionaires and billionaires and reshaping the global financial map.

The Financial Life Cycle: How Our Capitals Shape Our Decisions

An individual's financial journey is not static; it's a life-long evolution. We can think of this journey in distinct stages, each defined by shifts in our human capital, financial capital, and overall economic net worth. How we manage our money and the decisions we make are deeply influenced by which stage we're in.

In the early years of a career, typically from our 20s to early 40s, our human capital is at its peak. We have decades of potential earnings ahead of us. However, our financial capital is usually low. We might be paying off student loans, saving for a down payment on a house, and just beginning to build an investment portfolio. During this accumulation phase, our high human capital allows us to take on more investment risk. A market downturn is less terrifying because we have time and future income to recover losses. Financial decisions are focused on growth, career development to boost that human capital, and managing debt.

As we move into the mid-to-late career stage, from our 40s to our early 60s, a crucial shift occurs. Our human capital begins to decline as the years left to work dwindle. Simultaneously, our financial capital should be reaching its peak, thanks to years of saving, investing, and career progression. This is the consolidation phase. Financial decision-making becomes more balanced. While growth is still important, wealth preservation becomes a growing priority. We might start shifting our portfolio from aggressive growth stocks to more stable, income-producing assets. The focus is on paying down the mortgage, maximizing retirement contributions, and ensuring the nest egg is secure.

Finally, we enter the retirement or spending phase. At this point, human capital is largely depleted; we are no longer earning a regular salary. Our financial capital is now the primary source of our livelihood. Economic net worth may begin to decline as we draw down our savings to cover living expenses. Financial decisions in this stage are all about preservation and distribution. The primary objective is to make the money last. This means a low-risk investment strategy, focusing on generating a reliable income stream from dividends and interest. Estate planning, gifting, and philanthropic goals also become central to the financial conversation, ensuring a smooth transfer of wealth to the next generation or chosen causes.

Human and Financial Capital: The Bedrock of Investment Strategy

The interplay between human and financial capital is the cornerstone of personalized investment planning. It dictates everything from our return objectives and risk tolerance to the specific constraints that shape our portfolio. These two forms of capital act like a seesaw over our lifetime; as one goes down, the other typically goes up, and this dynamic should directly inform our investment strategy.

For a young investor with high human capital and low financial capital, the primary objective is aggressive growth. Their long time horizon and future earning power act as a buffer against market volatility. Essentially, their human capital is a stable, bond-like asset—a promise of future cash flows. To balance this, their financial portfolio can be heavily weighted towards riskier assets like stocks, which have higher expected returns. Their ability to take risks is high, and their need for liquidity (immediate cash) is generally lower. Constraints are minimal, often self-imposed, like saving for a specific goal.

Conversely, consider an individual nearing retirement. Their human capital is low, meaning their ability to earn their way out of a significant investment loss is limited. Their large pool of financial capital must now do all the work. As a result, their primary objective shifts from growth to capital preservation and income generation. Their tolerance for risk is, and should be, much lower. Their portfolio will naturally have a higher allocation to less volatile assets like high-quality bonds and dividend-paying stocks. Constraints become more prominent. They have a high need for liquidity to fund their lifestyle, and their time horizon for any single investment is much shorter. Their financial decisions are guided by the need to protect what they have built. An entrepreneur whose wealth is tied up in a single business has low-diversification financial capital, which would also be a major constraint, suggesting the rest of their portfolio should be exceptionally well-diversified and relatively conservative.

The Unseen Partners: How Taxes and Inflation Shape Investments

Every investor has two silent partners in their financial journey: taxes and inflation. Ignoring them is a recipe for disappointment, as they can significantly erode the real growth of a portfolio over time. Smart investment decisions are always made with a clear understanding of their impact.

Taxes are a direct and unavoidable cost of investing. Governments impose various taxes that can diminish returns. Capital gains taxes are levied on the profits you make when you sell an asset. Dividend taxes apply to the income paid out by stocks. Interest income from bonds is often taxed as regular income. The specific rates and rules vary dramatically by location and can change over time, making tax management a crucial part of wealth management. An investor might choose to hold an investment for over a year to qualify for a lower long-term capital gains rate. They might favor municipal bonds, whose interest is often tax-free. They might strategically sell losing investments to harvest tax losses, which can then be used to offset gains elsewhere in the portfolio, a practice known as tax-loss harvesting. The goal isn't to avoid taxes entirely, which is illegal, but to manage them intelligently to maximize after-tax returns.

Inflation is a more insidious force. It's the silent thief that reduces the purchasing power of your money. A 5% investment return might feel good, but if inflation is running at 3%, your real return—the actual increase in your buying power—is only 2%. If inflation exceeds your investment return, you are losing wealth in real terms even if your account balance is going up. This reality heavily influences investment decisions. Holding too much cash is a guaranteed way to lose purchasing power over the long term. Investments must be chosen for their potential to outpace inflation. This is why stocks and real estate, which have historically provided returns well above the rate of inflation, are essential components of a long-term portfolio. Inflation-protected securities, like TIPS (Treasury Inflation-Protected Securities), are another tool investors can use to directly hedge against this risk, ensuring their capital keeps pace with the rising cost of living.

Private vs. Institutional Clients: The Art of the Individualized Plan

The world of investment management serves two fundamentally different types of clients: private individuals and institutions. While both seek to grow their capital, their characteristics, objectives, and constraints are worlds apart, demanding distinct approaches.

Institutional clients are entities like pension funds, university endowments, insurance companies, and foundations. They are typically managed by committees and professional staff. Their defining features are a very long time horizon (often perpetual), a large asset base, and a high level of sophistication. Their objectives are often very specific and quantitatively driven, such as needing to earn an average of 7% per year to meet pension obligations. Their risk tolerance is high due to their scale and long-term nature. They are governed by complex regulations but are generally less influenced by personal emotions.

Private clients, on the other hand, are individuals and families. Their financial situation is deeply personal and often intertwined with complex emotions and unique life goals. Their time horizon is finite—it lasts their lifetime. While some may be incredibly wealthy, their asset base is smaller than a large institution's. Their objectives are often more qualitative and personal: "I want to retire comfortably," "I want to pay for my grandchildren's education," or "I want to leave a legacy." Their risk tolerance is not just a number; it's a reflection of their personality, past experiences, and anxieties. They are subject to personal income taxes, and their financial plan must account for life events like marriage, illness, and death.

This is why the Investment Policy Statement (IPS) is so critical for private clients. The IPS is a formal document that acts as the constitution for the client's portfolio. It's a bespoke blueprint formulated after deep discussions between the client and their advisor. It begins by defining the client's unique circumstances, goals, and objectives. It then quantifies their tolerance for risk, considering both their financial ability and their emotional willingness to withstand market downturns. The IPS outlines the client's constraints, including their time horizon, liquidity needs, tax situation, and any unique preferences, such as a desire to avoid investing in certain industries. Finally, it specifies the strategic asset allocation—the target mix of stocks, bonds, and other assets—that flows logically from all the preceding information. The IPS is a living document, but it provides the discipline and clarity needed to navigate market cycles and keep the client's personal financial journey on track.

Portfolio Management for Institutional Investors

Common Characteristics of Institutional Investors

Institutional investors are not your everyday, individual investors. They are large organizations that pool vast sums of money to invest on behalf of others. Think of pension funds, insurance companies, university endowments, and sovereign wealth funds. A primary characteristic they all share is scale. We're talking about managing billions, sometimes trillions, of dollars. This sheer size gives them significant advantages, such as access to investments that individuals can't get into, like private equity or complex derivatives. It also allows them to negotiate lower fees with investment managers, a small percentage that translates into massive savings given the capital involved.

Another key trait is their long-term perspective. Unlike an individual saving for a short-term goal, these institutions often have obligations stretching decades into the future. A pension fund, for instance, needs to pay retirees for the rest of their lives. This long horizon allows them to weather short-term market volatility and invest in assets that might take years to mature. Finally, they are governed by a formal and rigorous decision-making process. Investments aren't made on a whim. They are guided by a detailed investment policy statement and overseen by committees and boards of directors, bringing a level of discipline and professionalism that is central to their operations.

Investment Policy of Institutional Investors

The roadmap for any institutional investor is its Investment Policy Statement (IPS). This isn't just a guideline; it's a foundational document that dictates every investment decision. The IPS clearly lays out the fund's objectives and constraints. The primary objective is almost always to meet a specific set of future liabilities or spending needs. For a university endowment, it's about funding scholarships and research indefinitely. For an insurer, it's about being able to pay out claims.

The IPS also details the constraints the fund must operate within. This includes its tolerance for risk, liquidity needs (how much cash must be on hand), and any legal or regulatory rules it must follow. It will specify the asset allocation strategy—what percentage of the portfolio will be in stocks, bonds, real estate, and other asset classes. This strategic allocation is the most significant driver of long-term returns. The IPS serves as a crucial governance tool. It ensures continuity through changes in staff or committee members and provides a clear framework for evaluating the performance of the portfolio and its managers. It's the constitution by which the entire investment program abides.

Stakeholders, Liabilities, Time Horizons, and Liquidity

Each type of institutional investor serves a unique set of stakeholders and manages distinct liabilities, which in turn shapes their investment strategy.

Pension Funds: Their stakeholders are the employees (future retirees) and the sponsoring company. The primary liability is the stream of pension payments promised to these employees. This creates a very long time horizon, often 30 years or more. Liquidity needs are predictable, based on the retirement patterns of the workforce.

University Endowments: Stakeholders include current and future students, faculty, and the university itself. Their liability is to provide a steady stream of income to the university's operating budget in perpetuity. This creates an infinite time horizon. Liquidity needs are for the annual spending payout, which is a small percentage of the total fund.

Insurance Companies: Policyholders are the key stakeholders. Liabilities depend on the type of insurance. For a life insurer, liabilities are long-term and predictable. For a property and casualty insurer, they are shorter-term and highly unpredictable (tied to events like natural disasters). This means P&C insurers have much higher liquidity needs to pay out sudden, large claims.

Private Foundations: The stakeholders are the charitable causes the foundation supports. The liability is the mandated annual spending requirement (in the U.S., typically 5% of assets). Like endowments, they have a perpetual time horizon, but their liquidity needs are driven by this annual payout rule.

Legal, Regulatory, and Tax Constraints

Institutional investors operate within a complex web of rules. These constraints are not suggestions; they are hard limits that heavily influence portfolio construction. For pension funds in the U.S., the Employee Retirement Income Security Act (ERISA) is paramount. It imposes a "prudent person" standard, requiring fiduciaries to act with care and skill for the sole benefit of plan participants.

Foundations and endowments are generally tax-exempt, but they face regulations designed to ensure they fulfill their charitable missions. For example, private foundations must distribute a minimum portion of their assets each year to avoid penalties. Banks and insurance companies face the most stringent regulations. They are required to maintain specific levels of capital reserves to ensure solvency, which limits their ability to take on significant investment risk. Their portfolios are often heavily weighted towards high-quality, liquid bonds to match their liabilities and satisfy regulators. Sovereign wealth funds have varied constraints, often tied to national law and the fund's specific purpose, whether it's to save for future generations or stabilize the national budget.

Risk Considerations for Private Defined Benefit (DB) Pension Plans

Evaluating the risk of a private DB pension plan is a multifaceted exercise. The first key factor is the plan's funded status—the ratio of its assets to its liabilities. A plan that is underfunded (assets are less than liabilities) is inherently riskier and may need to take more investment risk to close the gap, creating a precarious situation. Second is the sponsor's financial strength. A strong, profitable company can afford to make contributions to shore up an underfunded plan. A struggling sponsor, however, poses a huge risk, as it may not be able to support the plan when needed.

Third, you must consider the interaction between the sponsor's business and the fund's investments. For example, a company in the oil and gas industry should be wary of having its pension plan heavily invested in energy stocks, as a downturn in the industry could hurt both the company's ability to contribute and the plan's assets simultaneously. The plan's design also matters. Features like early retirement options or cost-of-living adjustments can increase the size and uncertainty of liabilities. Finally, workforce characteristics are critical. A young, growing workforce means liabilities are far in the future, allowing for a longer investment horizon. An older, retired workforce means the plan is paying out benefits now, requiring higher liquidity and a more conservative investment approach.

Evaluating an Institutional Investor's Investment Policy Statement (IPS)

A strong IPS is the hallmark of a well-run institution. When evaluating one, you should look for several key elements. First, is it comprehensive and clear? It should state, without ambiguity, the fund's return objectives, risk tolerance, and all relevant constraints. A vague IPS is a red flag. The objectives should be specific and measurable, such as "achieve an annualized real return of 5% over a rolling ten-year period."

The asset allocation strategy should be well-defined, with clear target percentages for each asset class and allowable ranges around those targets. It should also specify the process and frequency for rebalancing the portfolio back to these targets. The IPS must also establish clear guidelines for monitoring and evaluating performance, including the benchmark that will be used to judge success. Finally, a robust IPS should be a living document. It should include provisions for how and when it will be reviewed and updated to reflect changes in the market, the institution's liabilities, or its risk tolerance. An IPS that is written and then forgotten is of little use.

Evaluating Investment Portfolios of Different Institutions

Evaluating the portfolio of an institutional investor requires understanding its unique context, as defined by its IPS.

Private DB Plan: A well-managed DB plan's portfolio will be closely tied to its liabilities. If the plan is mature with many retirees, you'd expect to see a higher allocation to long-duration bonds to match the predictable payout stream. A younger plan with an underfunded status might have a higher allocation to growth assets like global equities and private equity to try and generate higher returns.

Sovereign Wealth Fund (SWF): The portfolio depends on the SWF's purpose. A "stabilization fund" will be heavily invested in safe, liquid assets like government bonds to be ready to support the national budget during commodity price shocks. A "future generation fund," with an infinite horizon, will look more like an endowment, with a large allocation to global equities, real estate, and infrastructure to maximize long-term growth.

University Endowment: Given their perpetual time horizon and low liquidity needs, endowments are famous for pioneering high allocations to alternative investments. You would expect to see significant holdings in private equity, venture capital, and hedge funds, alongside a core of global equities. The goal is to generate high, equity-like returns over the very long run to preserve purchasing power after the annual payout.

Private Foundation: Its portfolio will resemble an endowment's but may be slightly more conservative. The mandatory 5% annual payout creates a constant liquidity need. This might lead to a slightly higher allocation to liquid assets like public equities and bonds compared to a large endowment, ensuring it can meet its spending obligations without being forced to sell illiquid assets at the wrong time.

Balance Sheet Management of Banks and Insurers

For banks and insurers, portfolio management is not just about generating returns; it's an exercise in managing their entire balance sheet. Their assets (the investment portfolio) must be managed in careful relation to their liabilities (deposits for banks, policy claims for insurers). This is known as asset-liability management (ALM).

Banks take in short-term deposits and make longer-term loans. Their investment portfolio, consisting of securities, must be managed to provide liquidity and manage interest rate risk. If rates rise, the value of their existing fixed-rate assets falls, and they may have to pay more for deposits. They use their investment portfolio to balance this duration mismatch.

Insurers have a similar challenge. They collect premiums today (assets) in exchange for promising to pay future claims (liabilities). For a life insurer with predictable long-term liabilities, the goal is to invest in long-duration bonds that match the timing of those payouts, locking in a spread. For a P&C insurer with unpredictable liabilities, the portfolio must be much more liquid, dominated by short-term, high-quality bonds to ensure they can pay claims from a major catastrophe without delay. In both cases, the investment portfolio's primary job is to ensure the institution remains solvent and can always meet its promises.

Trading Costs and Electronic Markets

Explaining the Components of Execution Costs

When you decide to buy or sell a stock, the final price you pay is rarely the exact price you saw on your screen at the moment of your decision. The total hit to your portfolio from making that trade is called the execution cost. Think of it like buying a car; there's the sticker price, and then there's the "out-the-door" price. Execution costs are the difference.

These costs are broken down into two main categories:

Explicit Costs: These are the visible, out-of-pocket expenses you can easily see on a brokerage statement. They are the fixed-price items on the receipt. They include things like brokerage commissions, exchange fees, and any clearing and settlement charges or taxes. They are straightforward and easy to account for.

Implicit Costs: These are the hidden, often more significant, costs. They aren't itemized on a bill but are just as real. The main types are the bid-ask spread (the difference between the highest price a buyer will pay and the lowest price a seller will accept), the market impact of your own trade (your large buy order pushing the price up), and the delay cost or slippage (the price moving against you in the time between your decision and the actual execution). There's also opportunity cost—the profit you missed out on because your trade couldn't be filled at all.

Calculating and Interpreting Spreads and VWAP Costs

To measure those tricky implicit costs, we use specific metrics. Two of the most common are the effective spread and VWAP analysis.

The effective spread gives you a much better picture of the actual liquidity cost than the simple bid-ask spread. It captures the price impact of your trade. For a buy order, the formula is:
Effective Spread=2×(Execution Price−Midpoint of the Quoted Spread)

A positive result means you paid more than the midpoint, which is typical. It tells you how much you paid for the immediacy of the trade. Interpreting it is simple: a lower effective spread means you got a better execution quality and paid less in implicit costs.

VWAP transaction cost estimation uses the Volume-Weighted Average Price (VWAP) as a benchmark. VWAP is the average price a security traded at throughout the day, based on both price and volume. If you're a buyer, your goal is to execute your trades at an average price below the day's VWAP. The cost is calculated as:
VWAP Cost (per share)=(Your Average Purchase Price−Security's VWAP)

If the result is positive, it means you paid more than the average trader that day, indicating a high transaction cost. If it's negative, you "beat" the benchmark.

The Implementation Shortfall Approach

Implementation shortfall is often considered the most comprehensive measure of transaction costs. It captures the total cost of an investment idea, from the moment the decision is made to the moment the final share is purchased. It's the difference between the value of a hypothetical "paper" portfolio where trades execute instantly at the decision price, and the value of your actual portfolio after the trade is completed.

Think of it this way: you decide to buy 10,000 shares when the price is $50.00. That's your "paper" portfolio. But by the time your broker finishes buying them all, the average price you paid was $50.05, and you paid $500 in commissions. The implementation shortfall measures that entire performance gap, including the price slippage, market impact, and explicit fees. It's the true cost of turning an idea into a reality.

Factors Driving the Development of Electronic Trading

The move from crowded trading floors with shouting traders to silent rooms of servers was driven by a perfect storm of factors. First and foremost was technology. The explosion in computing power and the expansion of high-speed data networks made it possible to process and transmit massive amounts of information almost instantly.

Regulation was another huge catalyst. For example, in the United States, Regulation NMS (National Market System) mandated that brokers must route orders to the venue with the best displayed price, forcing exchanges to compete electronically. This broke the dominance of traditional exchanges and spurred innovation. Finally, there was an intense pressure to lower costs. Automation is vastly cheaper than human labor, leading to drastically reduced commissions and making trading more accessible to everyone.

Describing Market Fragmentation

In the old days, if you wanted to trade a stock like IBM, you primarily went to one place: the New York Stock Exchange. Today, that is no longer the case. Market fragmentation means that trading in the very same stock now occurs across dozens of different venues simultaneously. These include traditional exchanges like the NYSE and NASDAQ, but also a growing number of Electronic Communication Networks (ECNs) and private trading venues known as "dark pools."

This fragmentation has pros and cons. On one hand, it fosters intense competition between trading venues, which helps drive down explicit trading fees. On the other hand, it splits liquidity, meaning the total pool of buyers and sellers is divided. This can sometimes make it harder to find the absolute best price without sophisticated technology that can scan all venues at once.

Identifying and Contrasting Types of Electronic Traders

The world of electronic trading isn't monolithic; it's populated by different players with very different goals.

High-Frequency Traders (HFTs) are the speed merchants. They use powerful computers and ultra-low-latency connections to execute millions of orders per day, aiming to profit from tiny, fleeting price discrepancies. Their strategies often involve market-making (simultaneously offering to buy and sell) or arbitrage.

Institutional Algorithmic Traders represent large institutions like pension funds or mutual funds. They aren't trying to make a quick buck on price wiggles. Instead, they use algorithms to execute very large orders over time with minimal market impact. Their goal is cost minimization, not speculative profit. They use strategies like VWAP algorithms to blend in with the market's natural volume.

Retail Traders are individuals like you and me, trading through online brokerage platforms. We are the beneficiaries of the technology, enjoying zero-commission trades and instant execution that was once the exclusive domain of professionals.

Characteristics and Uses of Electronic Trading Systems

Electronic trading systems are the tools that make all this possible. They come in several flavors.

Direct Market Access (DMA) systems give traders a high-speed pipeline directly to an exchange's matching engine, bypassing the slower, traditional brokerage route. This is all about minimizing latency for traders who need speed.

Algorithmic Trading Systems are platforms that allow users to deploy pre-programmed trading instructions. For example, a trader can instruct the system to buy 100,000 shares but to do so in small pieces, never accounting for more than 5% of the total market volume at any given time. Their primary use is to manage large orders, reduce human error, and execute complex strategies automatically.

Dark Pools are private electronic trading venues where order books are not visible to the public. Large institutions use them to trade massive blocks of stock without tipping off the market and causing the price to move against them before their order is complete.

Comparative Advantages of Low-Latency Traders

In electronic markets, speed is everything. Low-latency traders, primarily HFTs, gain their edge by being faster than everyone else, even by just microseconds. This speed gives them several key advantages.

First, they have an information advantage. They can process market data feeds and react to new information (like an earnings release or a news headline) before other market participants can even read it. Second, they have an execution advantage. By being first in the queue to place an order at a new price, they can capture a profitable spread or arbitrage opportunity before it disappears. This speed allows them to act as market makers, providing the liquidity that keeps markets running smoothly, while profiting from the bid-ask spread.

Risks of Electronic Trading and How Regulators Mitigate Them

The incredible speed and automation of electronic trading also introduce new and potent risks. The primary concern is systemic risk, where a single malfunctioning algorithm could trigger a cascade of selling, leading to a "flash crash" where market prices plummet in minutes for no fundamental reason. There is also operational risk, such as a "fat-finger" error where a trader accidentally enters an order for a billion shares instead of a million, or the risk of cyberattacks.

Regulators have implemented several safeguards to mitigate these dangers. Market-wide circuit breakers will halt all trading for a short period if major indices fall too quickly. "Kill switches" are now mandatory for firms, giving them the ability to immediately shut down any trading algorithm that appears to be behaving erratically. Finally, rules like the SEC's Market Access Rule require brokerage firms to have pre-trade risk controls in place to vet orders for size and price before they can ever hit the market.

Abusive Trading Practices Detected by Surveillance

With every technological advance comes new ways to try and cheat the system. Modern market surveillance is designed to detect these abusive electronic trading practices in real-time.

Spoofing is the act of placing a large, visible order with no intention of letting it execute. The goal is to trick other traders into thinking there is real buying or selling interest, which moves the price. The spoofer then cancels the fake order and trades in the opposite direction to profit from the price change they induced.

Layering is a more complex version of spoofing, involving multiple fake orders at different price levels to create a false impression of liquidity.

Quote Stuffing involves flooding the market with an enormous number of orders and cancellations to clog the system, distracting or slowing down competitors while the abuser carries out their strategy on a different venue. This is like a denial-of-service attack on the market itself.

Case Study in Portfolio Management: Institutional (SWF)

Case Study in Portfolio Management: The Althara Sovereign Wealth Fund

Introduction

Imagine a nation, Althara, blessed with abundant natural resources. For decades, its economy thrived on the export of these resources. To secure the nation's future prosperity long after the resources have been depleted, the government establishes the Althara Sovereign Wealth Fund (ASWF). The fund's mandate is twofold: to generate stable, long-term returns to support future generations and to contribute to the nation's economic diversification. The ASWF's strategy involves significant long-term direct investments in global infrastructure, renewable energy projects, and innovative technology companies. While this strategy promises substantial rewards, it also exposes the fund to a complex web of financial and non-financial risks.
Financial Risks in the Portfolio Strategy

The ASWF's ambitious strategy is not without its financial perils. One of the most significant is market risk. The fund's global investments mean it's exposed to the ups and downs of international stock markets, interest rate fluctuations, and currency exchange volatility. A sudden economic downturn in a region where the ASWF has heavily invested could lead to substantial portfolio losses. For example, their large stake in a European high-speed rail project could see its valuation plummet if the Euro weakens or the continent slips into recession. The very nature of being a global investor means the ASWF cannot insulate itself from worldwide economic shifts.

Then there is liquidity risk. Many of the ASWF's direct investments, such as infrastructure projects, are inherently illiquid. Unlike public stocks that can be sold in an instant, selling a stake in a toll road or a wind farm can take months, or even years, and may require selling at a discount. If Althara faces an unexpected domestic crisis and needs to access the fund's capital quickly, the ASWF might struggle to liquidate these assets without incurring significant financial penalties. This long-term investment horizon, while beneficial for growth, creates a potential cash-flow bottleneck.

Furthermore, credit risk is a constant concern. When the ASWF invests in corporate bonds or provides loans to its direct investment projects, there's always the chance that the borrower will default on their payments. Imagine the fund has financed a cutting-edge biotech firm. While the potential returns from a medical breakthrough are enormous, so is the risk of the company failing and being unable to repay its debt. The ASWF must conduct rigorous due diligence, but in the world of long-term, innovative projects, uncertainties always remain.

Environmental and Social Risks

Beyond the balance sheets, the ASWF faces profound environmental risks. A significant portion of its portfolio is dedicated to infrastructure and renewable energy. A direct investment in a coastal port facility, for instance, is exposed to the physical risks of climate change, such as rising sea levels and more frequent extreme weather events. A hurricane could damage the infrastructure, leading to costly repairs and business interruption, directly impacting the fund's returns. Similarly, transition risks are a major factor. As the world moves towards a low-carbon economy, investments in companies that are slow to adapt could become "stranded assets." A stake in a company heavily reliant on fossil fuels for its supply chain, for example, could lose value as carbon taxes are implemented or consumer preferences shift towards greener alternatives.

Social risks are equally critical to the ASWF's reputation and long-term success. Direct investments in large-scale projects in developing nations can be fraught with social complexities. The fund might invest in a mining operation that, despite promising economic benefits to the host country, faces accusations of poor labor practices or displacing local communities. Such a controversy can lead to protests, operational disruptions, and severe reputational damage. In the age of social media, a single negative story can go viral, tarnishing the ASWF's image as a responsible global investor and potentially leading to divestment campaigns or political pressure back home. The social license to operate is a very real, albeit intangible, asset.

Finally, there's the overarching governance risk. This encompasses how well the companies the ASWF invests in are managed. Weak corporate governance, characterized by a lack of transparency, corruption, or a disregard for shareholder rights, can destroy value. If the ASWF invests in a tech startup with a brilliant product but a dysfunctional board of directors, the likelihood of that company reaching its full potential is significantly diminished. The fund must ensure its portfolio companies adhere to high ethical and operational standards.

Analysis and Evaluation of Risk Exposures

To truly understand its vulnerabilities, the ASWF needs to conduct a holistic analysis of these exposures. The financial risks, while complex, can often be quantified. The fund can use sophisticated financial models like Value at Risk (VaR) to estimate potential portfolio losses under various market scenarios. Stress testing can simulate how the portfolio would perform during a global financial crisis or a sudden spike in oil prices. For credit risk, the fund relies on credit rating agencies and its own internal analysis to assess the default probability of its investments.

Evaluating non-financial risks is more qualitative but no less important. For environmental risks, the ASWF can conduct climate scenario analysis to model the potential impact of global warming on its physical assets. It can also use ESG (Environmental, Social, and Governance) rating agencies to screen potential investments and monitor the performance of its existing portfolio companies. For social risks, the fund needs to engage in on-the-ground due diligence, consulting with local communities and NGOs before investing in sensitive projects. This involves understanding the local culture, political landscape, and potential sources of social friction.

The key is to see how these risks interconnect. A severe drought (environmental risk) in an agricultural region could lead to a company defaulting on its loan (credit risk), which in turn impacts the fund's overall market performance (market risk). The ASWF's analysis must move beyond silos and embrace an integrated view of risk, recognizing that a problem in one area can easily cascade into others. The evaluation isn't a one-time event; it's a continuous process of monitoring, reassessment, and adaptation.

Managing Risks in Long-Term Direct Investments

Managing these multifaceted risks requires a proactive and diversified toolkit. For financial risks, hedging is a primary strategy. The ASWF can use derivatives like currency futures to protect against foreign exchange fluctuations or interest rate swaps to manage interest rate risk. While hedging can be costly, it provides a crucial buffer against market volatility. Diversification is another cornerstone of risk management. By spreading its investments across different geographic regions, asset classes, and industries, the ASWF can ensure that a negative event in one area doesn't cripple the entire portfolio.

For non-financial risks, active ownership is paramount. Instead of being a passive investor, the ASWF can use its position as a major shareholder to influence corporate behavior. This can involve engaging in dialogue with company management on ESG issues, voting on shareholder resolutions, and even seeking board representation. By actively pushing its portfolio companies to improve their environmental practices and social responsibility, the ASWF not only mitigates risk but can also unlock long-term value.

Co-investing with reputable partners is another effective strategy. By partnering with other institutional investors or development banks with strong track records in specific regions or sectors, the ASWF can share the risks and benefit from the local expertise and due diligence of its partners. Finally, purchasing insurance for specific risks, such as political risk insurance for investments in unstable countries or property insurance for infrastructure assets, provides a direct financial backstop against potential losses.

Evaluating and Improving the Enterprise Risk Management (ERM) System

Let's assume the ASWF has an existing Enterprise Risk Management (ERM) system. A key strength of its current system is a robust framework for identifying and quantifying financial risks. It has a dedicated team of quantitative analysts and uses industry-standard software for market and credit risk analysis. However, a significant weakness is its handling of non-financial risks. The ESG analysis is largely a box-ticking exercise, relying on third-party data without deep, qualitative investigation. The social risk assessment is often done late in the investment process and doesn't adequately involve stakeholder engagement.

To improve, the ASWF should first integrate ESG factors into the core of the investment decision-making process, not as an afterthought. Every investment proposal should include a detailed analysis of environmental and social risks and opportunities, with clear metrics for success. This requires training investment teams to think like sustainability experts.

Second, the fund needs to enhance its stakeholder engagement capabilities. This means building relationships with local communities, governments, and civil society organizations in the regions where it invests. Creating formal channels for feedback and grievance mechanisms can help identify and resolve social issues before they escalate into major crises.

Finally, the ASWF should develop a more sophisticated approach to scenario analysis that incorporates non-financial factors. What is the impact of a global pandemic on its supply chains? How would a widespread water shortage affect its agricultural investments? By modeling these "black swan" events, the fund can build a more resilient and future-proof portfolio. The ultimate goal is to foster a true risk culture throughout the organization, where every employee, from the CEO to the junior analyst, understands their role in managing the complex risks that come with securing the prosperity of an entire nation.

Chapter 3: Performance Measurement

Portfolio Performance Evaluation

The Three Pillars of Portfolio Evaluation: Measurement, Attribution, and Appraisal

Understanding how a portfolio performed is much more than just looking at the final return figure. It's a deep dive, a story told in three parts. Think of it as a complete diagnostic check-up for an investment strategy. The three core components of this process are performance measurement, performance attribution, and performance appraisal. They are not isolated steps; instead, they flow logically from one to the next, each building upon the last to provide a complete picture.

Performance Measurement: The "What'

This is the starting line. Performance measurement is the most straightforward part of the evaluation, as it simply answers the question: "What was the portfolio's return?" It's the process of calculating the quantitative performance of an investment portfolio over a specific period. This involves computing the rate of return, which could be a simple holding period return or more complex calculations like time-weighted or money-weighted rates of return, especially when cash flows are involved. It's the raw data, the scoreboard. For example, a measurement might reveal that a portfolio returned 12% over the last year. This number, on its own, is just a fact. It doesn't tell us if 12% was good or bad, nor does it explain how that 12% was achieved. It is the fundamental building block upon which all further analysis rests. Without an accurate measurement of what happened, any attempt to understand why it happened would be pure guesswork.

Performance Attribution: The "Why"

Once we know what the return was, the very next question is why we got that return. This is the job of performance attribution. It is the investigative phase, the part where we dissect the measured performance to identify the sources of that return. Did the returns come from brilliant stock picking? Was it because the manager made a smart bet on a particular sector, like technology or healthcare? Or was it due to a strategic decision to be heavily invested in stocks when the market was soaring? Attribution breaks down the portfolio's excess return (the return above a chosen benchmark) into its key drivers, such as asset allocation and security selection. For instance, our 12% return might have come in a year when the benchmark only returned 10%. Attribution would help us figure out how much of that 2% outperformance came from choosing the right market sectors versus picking the winning stocks within those sectors.

Performance Appraisal: The "So What?"

Finally, we arrive at performance appraisal. We know the portfolio returned 12% (measurement), and we know that this return was driven primarily by successful stock selection (attribution). The ultimate question now is, "So what?" Was this performance good enough? Was it the result of genuine skill, or was the manager just lucky? Performance appraisal seeks to answer this. It evaluates the quality of the investment decisions. This step involves using risk-adjusted performance measures, such as the Sharpe ratio, Treynor ratio, or Jensen's alpha, which consider the level of risk taken to achieve the return. A manager who delivers a 12% return by taking on an enormous amount of risk might be appraised less favorably than a manager who achieved an 11% return with very low risk. Appraisal, therefore, is the final judgment. It concludes whether the manager added value through repeatable skill, providing crucial feedback for future investment decisions. The interrelationship is a clear, linear path: We measure the result, attribute the causes, and then appraise the quality of the decisions that led to it.

The Hallmarks of an Effective Attribution Process

A performance attribution analysis is only as good as the process behind it. A flawed process can lead to misleading conclusions, causing investors to fire skilled managers or reward lucky ones. To be truly effective and trustworthy, an attribution process must possess several key attributes that ensure its results are not just numbers on a page, but a reliable tool for decision-making.

First and foremost, an effective attribution process must be unambiguous and transparent. The methodology should be clear and well-defined. Anyone reviewing the analysis, whether it's a client or a senior investment officer, should be able to understand exactly how the results were derived. There shouldn't be any "black box" elements where the inputs go in and the conclusions come out with no clear explanation of the transformation. This clarity builds trust and allows for meaningful conversations about performance.

Secondly, the process must be accurate and based on timely data. This sounds obvious, but it is a critical foundation. The analysis must use precise portfolio holdings, correct transaction data, and appropriate benchmark information. Garbage in, garbage out. If the input data is flawed or stale, the attribution results will be meaningless. A robust system relies on clean, validated data that is captured and processed promptly to reflect the portfolio's reality.

Another crucial attribute is consistency. The attribution methodology should be applied consistently over time and across all portfolios being evaluated. You can't compare apples to oranges. If the rules of the game change from one quarter to the next, it becomes impossible to identify trends, evaluate a manager's long-term skill, or fairly compare one manager to another. Consistency provides a stable framework for evaluation.

Furthermore, a great attribution process is exhaustive. The components of attribution—such as allocation, selection, and perhaps currency effects—must fully explain the difference between the portfolio's return and the benchmark's return. There shouldn't be a large, unexplained "other" or "residual" category. If a significant portion of the performance is left unexplained, the analysis has failed in its primary purpose of identifying the key drivers of returns.

Finally, the results must be meaningful and relevant to the investment process itself. The analysis should reflect the manager's actual investment philosophy and decision-making structure. For example, if a manager is purely a bottom-up stock picker who doesn't make sector bets, an attribution model that heavily focuses on sector allocation effects might not provide useful insights. The framework should align with how decisions are truly made, providing actionable feedback that can help refine and improve the investment strategy going forward.

Contrasting Key Attribution Frameworks

Within the world of performance attribution, different lenses can be used to analyze a portfolio's journey. These frameworks help us understand performance from different angles, focusing on either the sources of return or the sources of risk, and looking from either a high-level strategic viewpoint or a detailed, manager-specific perspective.

Return Attribution vs. Risk Attribution

The most fundamental contrast lies between return and risk attribution. While they sound similar, they are asking two very different, yet equally important, questions about the portfolio.

Return attribution is historical and backward-looking. Its entire purpose is to explain what happened to the portfolio's return in the past. It deconstructs the realized performance—the gains and losses that have already occurred—and assigns them to specific decisions. For example, it might conclude that "positive stock selection in the technology sector added 0.50% to the portfolio's outperformance last quarter." It is focused on the sources of profit.

Risk attribution, on the other hand, is forward-looking and concerned with potential outcomes. It doesn't focus on past returns but on the portfolio's volatility and its exposure to various risk factors. It answers the question, "Where does the portfolio's risk come from?" It dissects the portfolio's total risk (often measured by standard deviation or tracking error) and attributes it to different factors, such as exposure to interest rate risk, market risk, or credit risk. A risk attribution report might state that "40% of the portfolio's active risk is driven by its overweight position in emerging market equities." It is focused on the sources of potential volatility and loss. In essence, return attribution explains the past, while risk attribution helps manage the future.

Macro vs. Micro Return Attribution

Another key contrast is between macro and micro attribution, which represents a top-down versus a bottom-up view of performance. This distinction is vital for large investment funds, like pension plans or endowments, where decisions are made at multiple levels.

Macro attribution takes a bird's-eye view. It evaluates the high-level policy decisions made by the fund's sponsors or board of trustees. These are the big, strategic choices. The analysis starts at the very top by examining the impact of the overall investment policy, specifically the long-term asset allocation decision (e.g., the decision to have 60% in stocks, 30% in bonds, and 10% in real estate). It then might analyze the contribution of different asset class managers to the total fund performance. It's about judging the effectiveness of the overarching investment strategy.

Micro attribution, in contrast, zooms in to analyze the performance of a single portfolio manager operating within one of those asset classes. It seeks to answer, "Given a specific mandate (e.g., to manage a U.S. large-cap growth stock portfolio), how well did the manager do?" This analysis focuses on the manager's specific value-add through security selection (which stocks they bought) and sector or factor timing (when they were overweight or underweight certain industries). Micro attribution is about judging the skill of the individual manager in executing their specific strategy. Together, they provide a complete hierarchical view of performance, from the boardroom to the trading desk.

The Three Methods of Performance Attribution

To actually perform the calculations behind attribution, analysts primarily turn to one of three methodologies:

returns-based, holdings-based, or transactions-based attribution. Each method uses a different level of data granularity, and as a result, each comes with its own distinct set of advantages and disadvantages. Choosing the right one often depends on data availability, cost, and the required level of precision.

Returns-Based Attribution

This is the least data-intensive approach. Returns-based attribution uses only the portfolio's total periodic returns (e.g., monthly returns) and the corresponding returns of various market style indices (like large-cap growth, small-cap value, etc.). Through a statistical process like multiple regression, the analysis finds the combination of indices that best explains the historical return pattern of the portfolio.

Advantages: Its biggest advantage is its simplicity and low cost. It doesn't require any information about the actual securities held in the portfolio, making it easy to apply to funds where holdings are not disclosed, like hedge funds or mutual funds. You only need the stream of returns.

Disadvantages: This method is essentially an educated guess. It reveals what the portfolio behaved like, not what it actually did. It is an approximation and can be very inaccurate if a manager's style drifts over time. Furthermore, it provides no insight into specific securities, making it impossible to identify the impact of individual winning or losing stocks.

Holdings-Based Attribution

Taking a step up in data requirements, holdings-based attribution analyzes a portfolio's performance using periodic snapshots of its holdings—typically at the beginning and end of a month or quarter. It compares the securities held in the portfolio at a point in time against the constituents of a benchmark. The analysis then calculates the contribution from security selection and asset allocation based on the difference in weightings and the performance of those assets over the period.

Advantages: This is far more accurate than returns-based analysis because it uses the actual securities held by the manager. It provides valuable insight into the manager's intended strategy and positioning at specific points in time. It's a popular middle ground that offers good detail without being excessively burdensome.

Disadvantages: Its main weakness is that it's blind to what happens between the snapshots. It completely misses the impact of any intraday or intra-period trading. A manager could buy a stock, see it rise 20%, and sell it for a profit all within the same month. If that stock isn't held at the start or end of the month, holdings-based attribution would never see this successful trade.

Transactions-Based Attribution

This is the most precise and detailed method available—the gold standard of attribution. Transactions-based attribution incorporates every single transaction (every buy, sell, dividend, and interest payment) that occurs within the portfolio. It tracks the portfolio's composition in real-time. By valuing the portfolio daily and analyzing each transaction, it can precisely link every bit of performance to specific decisions.

Advantages: It is perfectly accurate. It captures the exact impact of every decision made by the portfolio manager, including the timing of trades. There is no ambiguity and no residual "unexplained" factor. It provides a complete and true accounting of how the manager generated returns.

Disadvantages: The precision comes at a high price. This method requires a vast amount of clean, detailed, and timely data. Implementing and maintaining the systems to process this data can be very expensive and complex. For many organizations, the marginal benefit in accuracy may not justify the significant increase in cost and operational complexity over a well-executed holdings-based approach.

Interpreting the Sources of Portfolio Returns

So, your portfolio went up 10% last year. That's great news! But the real question is, why? Was it pure luck, or was your investment manager making brilliant decisions? This is where return attribution comes in. Think of it as an autopsy of your portfolio's performance, carefully dissecting the results to understand what worked and what didn't. It's all about separating skill from luck.

One of the most classic ways to do this is through an approach that breaks performance down into two main buckets: asset allocation and security selection.

First, let's talk about asset allocation. This is the big-picture decision. It's about how much of your money you decide to put into major categories like stocks, bonds, real estate, and so on. Let's say your manager decided to put more money into stocks than their benchmark suggested because they felt bullish about the economy. If stocks then had a fantastic year, that decision to overweight stocks was a winning move. That positive impact is the "allocation effect." It's the return you get from being in the right place at the right time.

Second, we have security selection. This is the nitty-gritty, stock-picking part of the job. Within that bucket of stocks, did your manager pick the high-flyers like Apple and NVIDIA, or did they pick the ones that went nowhere? If the specific stocks your manager chose did better than the average stock in the market index, that success is credited to security selection. It's a measure of the manager's skill in finding individual winners within a given asset class.

When you get an attribution report, you'll see these effects quantified. It might say something like: "Your excess return of 2% was composed of a +1.5% allocation effect and a +0.5% selection effect." Interpreting this is simple: your manager added the most value through their big-picture market calls (allocation), and they also added a smaller, but still positive, amount of value by picking good stocks (selection). This helps you understand your manager's true strengths.

Interpreting Fixed-Income Attribution Analyses

Now, let's switch gears to the world of bonds. Trying to figure out where returns came from in a fixed-income portfolio is a bit like being a detective at a different kind of crime scene. The clues are totally different from the equity world. Instead of just picking winning companies, bond managers are dealing with the complex dance of interest rates, credit quality, and time.

When you look at a fixed-income attribution report, you're not going to see the same simple "allocation" and "selection" buckets. Instead, the output will highlight the unique drivers of bond returns. A major one is the yield curve effect. The yield curve is just a graph showing interest rates across different loan periods (maturities). It almost never stays still. If the entire curve shifts down (interest rates fall), your bonds generally go up in value. The report will tell you how much of your return came from this overall market movement. It can get even more specific, breaking it down into how your portfolio was affected by a twist in the curve (short-term and long-term rates moving differently) or changes in its curvature. Interpreting this tells you if your manager's bets on the direction of interest rates paid off.

Another huge factor is spread analysis, which is the bond world's version of security selection. This looks at credit risk. Corporate bonds, for example, pay a higher yield (a "spread") over super-safe government bonds to compensate for the risk of default. If your manager buys a bond from a company and that company's financial health improves, its spread will tighten, and the bond's price will rise. A positive number in this category on your report means your manager was skilled at identifying bonds that became more valuable relative to the market.

Finally, for portfolios that invest globally, you'll see a currency effect. If your manager bought a bond denominated in Euros and the Euro strengthened against the US dollar, you made extra money just from the currency translation. The attribution report isolates this effect, so you can see if your manager is adding value through savvy currency bets or if foreign exchange movements are hurting your returns. In short, interpreting these outputs is about understanding if the manager won by navigating interest rates, picking the right credit risks, or making smart currency calls.

Considerations in Selecting a Risk Attribution Approach

Choosing how to analyze your portfolio's risk is a lot like choosing the right diagnostic tool for a patient. A simple stethoscope might be fine for a check-up, but you might need an MRI for a more complex problem. There isn't a single "best" risk attribution approach for everyone; the right choice depends entirely on the situation.

One of the first big considerations is deciding between a factor-based approach versus a simpler asset-based one. An asset-based approach is straightforward: it tells you how much risk is coming from your stocks, how much from your bonds, and so on. It's easy to understand. A factor-based approach digs much deeper. It slices your risk into underlying drivers that span across asset classes, such as your portfolio's sensitivity to economic growth, inflation, interest rates, or market volatility. If your goal is a deep, fundamental understanding of what makes your portfolio tick, a factor model is powerful. But this leads to the next consideration.

That consideration is the trade-off between complexity and interpretability. A highly sophisticated, multi-factor risk model might be technically brilliant, but if the portfolio managers and the investment committee can't understand its output, it's useless. The report can't just be a black box that spits out numbers. The chosen approach must produce insights that are intuitive and, most importantly, actionable. Sometimes, a simpler model that everyone understands and trusts is far more effective than a complex one that nobody does.

You also have to be brutally honest about your data availability and quality. Advanced risk models are hungry for data—and it has to be clean, accurate, and available over a long history. If you don't have the necessary data infrastructure, trying to implement a complex model will lead to a classic "garbage in, garbage out" scenario. Your results will be unreliable and misleading.

Finally, the best risk attribution models are those that align with the actual investment process. If your manager is a bottom-up stock picker who thinks in terms of company fundamentals, a risk model that only talks about macroeconomic factors might not resonate with them. The tool should speak the same language as the user. It should reflect how they think about risk so that it can help them build a better, more resilient portfolio.

Asset Owner vs. Investment Manager Results

In the world of large-scale investing, like a pension fund or a university endowment, there are two key players: the asset owner and the investment manager. Figuring out who is responsible for what portion of the investment results is absolutely critical for good governance and clear accountability. It's about giving credit where credit is due.

The asset owner is the entity that ultimately holds the funds—think of them as the architect of the entire investment plan. Their most important job is setting the Strategic Asset Allocation (SAA), also known as the policy portfolio. This is the long-term, foundational blueprint for the fund. For example, the pension board (the asset owner) might decide on a policy of holding 60% in global stocks, 30% in bonds, and 10% in real estate. This single decision is usually the most significant driver of long-term returns. The performance of this basic, do-nothing policy portfolio is the result attributable directly to the asset owner. If that 60/30/10 mix was a brilliant choice for the economic climate over the past decade, the board deserves the credit for that success.

The investment manager, on the other hand, is the specialist hired to implement the plan. Think of them as the builder executing the architect's blueprint. Their performance is measured by the value they add on top of the policy portfolio they were assigned. This "value-add" or "active return" is what they are paid for, and it comes from two primary activities. The first is tactical asset allocation. This involves making short-term shifts away from the long-term policy. For instance, if the manager thinks stocks are poised for a short-term rally, they might temporarily shift their portfolio to be 65% stocks instead of the 60% policy target. If they're right, that extra 5% in stocks generates a return that is clearly attributable to the manager's skill.

The second activity is security selection. Within the 65% they allocated to stocks, did they pick stocks that beat the stock market index? That outperformance is also part of their value-add. So, when we interpret the results, we can say, "The total return was 11%. Of that, 9% came from the policy benchmark set by the asset owner. The additional 2% was the value added by the manager, which came from their tactical bets and superior stock picking." This separation is beautiful because it creates perfect clarity.

Discussing the Uses of Liability-Based Benchmarks

For most people, a benchmark is something familiar like the S&P 500. The goal is simple: beat the index. But for certain institutions, like pension plans or insurance companies, that's not the main goal at all. Their primary objective isn't to beat the market; it's to make sure they have enough money to pay their future promises, or liabilities. This is where a completely different kind of yardstick, the liability-based benchmark, comes into play.

A liability-based benchmark is a custom-built portfolio designed to mimic the behavior of an organization's future obligations. For a pension plan, those liabilities are the pension checks they will have to send to retirees for decades to come. The value of these future payments changes with factors like interest rates and inflation. So, a liability-based benchmark is constructed to move in lockstep with the value of those liabilities.

The most important use of this benchmark is for Asset-Liability Management (ALM). It's all about managing the assets and liabilities together, not in isolation. The goal is to minimize the risk of a shortfall, where the assets are not enough to cover the promises made. By measuring the asset portfolio against a benchmark that behaves just like the liabilities, a pension fund can see if they are on track. If the assets go up 5% but the liabilities (and the benchmark) go up 7%, they know they have lost ground and their funding gap has widened, even if they beat the S&P 500.

This naturally leads to its use in risk management. The true risk for a pension fund isn't market volatility; it's the risk of not being able to pay pensioners. A liability-based benchmark forces the investment manager to focus on managing the risks that actually matter to the liabilities, like interest rate risk. For example, if interest rates fall, the value of future pension payments goes up significantly. The manager needs to hold assets (like long-term bonds) that will also go up in that environment to hedge this risk.

Finally, it provides a far more appropriate tool for performance evaluation. Judging a pension manager against the S&P 500 is like judging a marathon runner on their swimming speed—it's the wrong contest. A manager's success should be defined by their ability to generate returns over and above the growth rate of the liabilities. Using a liability-based benchmark aligns everyone—the asset owner and the manager—around the true mission of the fund: securing the promised benefits.

Types of Asset-Based Benchmarks

Think of a benchmark as a yardstick. If you're a fund manager, it's the standard you're measured against. It's the answer to the simple but crucial question: "How did you do?" But not all yardsticks are the same. Picking the right one is absolutely critical, and that's why several types have been developed over the years, each with its own purpose.

The most straightforward type is an absolute return benchmark. This is as simple as it gets. The goal might be to earn, say, 8% per year, or to beat inflation by 5%. It's a fixed target. This sounds great because it's easy to understand, but it has a major weakness. It completely ignores what the market is doing. If the entire stock market crashes by 30% and your manager only loses 5%, they've done a phenomenal job. But against an 8% absolute benchmark, they look like a failure. It lacks context.

To solve that problem, we have the most common type: broad market indexes. You've definitely heard of these. The S&P 500, the Dow Jones Industrial Average, or the MSCI World Index are perfect examples. These indexes represent the performance of an entire market or a large segment of it. So, if a manager's job is to invest in large U.S. stocks, comparing them to the S&P 500 makes a lot of sense. It tells you if they were able to beat the average performance of the market they operate in. It provides that missing context.

But even broad indexes aren't perfect. What if your manager has a specific specialty? Maybe they only invest in fast-growing tech companies or in undervalued, forgotten "value" stocks. Comparing them to the entire S&P 500 isn't quite fair, because it includes all sorts of companies. This is where style indexes come in. Think of these as more refined, specialized versions of the broad indexes. For example, you have the Russell 1000 Growth Index and the Russell 1000 Value Index. These allow you to compare a growth manager to other growth stocks, and a value manager to other value stocks. It's a much more apples-to-apples comparison.

Finally, for the most tailored situations, we have custom or blended benchmarks. Imagine a balanced fund that is required to hold 60% stocks and 40% bonds. It would be unfair to compare it to a 100% stock index or a 100% bond index. The solution? You create a custom benchmark by "blending" the two. You could build a yardstick that is 60% of the S&P 500's return and 40% of the Bloomberg U.S. Aggregate Bond Index's return. This perfectly reflects the fund's own unique strategy and is often considered the most accurate way to measure a manager's true skill.

Tests of Benchmark Quality

So, we have these different types of benchmarks. But what separates a good one from a bad one? You can't just pick any old index and call it a day. A properly constructed benchmark needs to pass a series of common-sense tests. A great benchmark is valid, and a bad one can hide poor performance or make an average manager look like a superstar. There are several key criteria that a quality benchmark must meet.

First and foremost, a benchmark must be specified in advance. This is non-negotiable. You have to decide on the yardstick before the measurement period begins. Why? Because if you wait until after you see the results, you could be tempted to pick the benchmark that makes you look best. Imagine a runner finishing a race, and only then does the judge draw the finish line behind them. It would be meaningless. The same principle applies here; the rules of the game must be set beforehand.

Next, a benchmark has to be appropriate. It must reflect the manager's investment style and universe. If you hire a manager to invest in European stocks, you can't measure them against the S&P 500, which tracks U.S. stocks. That's like judging a baker on their ability to fix a car. The benchmark should represent the decisions the manager has. It should be a true reflection of their playground.

It also needs to be measurable. The benchmark's return should be easy to calculate and available on a regular basis. You need to know the score. A benchmark whose value is mysterious or only calculated once a year is not very useful for ongoing performance evaluation. It must be transparent and readily available to all parties. Similarly, it must be unambiguous; the components and weights of the securities in the benchmark should be clearly defined.

A surprisingly important test is whether the benchmark is investable. Can you, theoretically, put your money into the benchmark and get the benchmark's return? For something like the S&P 500, the answer is a resounding yes—you can just buy an S&P 500 index fund or ETF. This is a crucial test because it establishes the benchmark as a legitimate alternative to the actively managed portfolio. If the manager can't beat a simple, low-cost index fund that mirrors the benchmark, then why are you paying them higher fees?

Finally, the manager must be accountable for the benchmark. This means they are aware of it and accept it as the standard by which their success will be judged. A quality benchmark is a fair and honest measure that both the client and the manager agree upon from the start.

Impact of Benchmark Misspecification on Analysis

Picking the wrong benchmark—what we call "benchmark misspecification"—isn't just a small mistake. It can completely poison the well of investment analysis, leading to dangerously wrong conclusions about a fund manager's skill. It distorts the two main pillcrs of performance evaluation: appraisal and attribution.

Let's start with performance appraisal. This is the process of judging a manager. Did they add value? Are they worth the fees they charge? The most common way to measure this is by calculating their "alpha" (α). Alpha is the return they generated above and beyond the benchmark's return, adjusted for risk. If you use the wrong benchmark, the alpha calculation becomes pure fiction.

Imagine a manager who invests in risky, small-cap tech stocks. If you mistakenly compare them to a benchmark of slow-and-steady U.S. Treasury bonds, their returns will look astronomical. You'll calculate a huge, positive alpha and conclude that the manager is a genius. In reality, they just took on a ton more risk, and you simply used the wrong yardstick to measure them. This is a "false positive." The opposite is also true. A conservative manager measured against a high-flying, inappropriate benchmark might show a negative alpha and get fired, even if they did an excellent job of preserving capital, which was their actual goal. The appraisal becomes meaningless.

The impact is just as damaging for attribution analysis. Attribution goes a step deeper than appraisal. It doesn't just ask, "Did you win?" It asks, "How and why did you win?" It breaks down a manager's performance into its key drivers, such as their ability to pick the right stocks (security selection) or their decision to overweight certain sectors (asset allocation).

When the benchmark is misspecified, this entire diagnostic process goes haywire. For example, let's say a fund's official benchmark is the S&P 500, but the manager has a clear and consistent bias towards "growth" stocks. If growth stocks have a great year, the attribution model will wrongly praise the manager for their brilliant "stock selection." In reality, their outperformance had little to do with picking individual stocks and everything to do with their permanent "style tilt" towards growth—a tilt that the S&P 500 benchmark doesn't account for. You end up rewarding (or punishing) them for the wrong reasons, completely misunderstanding the true source of their performance.

Problems in Benchmarking Alternative Investments

If benchmarking traditional stocks and bonds is a challenge, then benchmarking alternative investments is like navigating a maze in the dark. Alternative investments—things like private equity, venture capital, hedge funds, real estate, and infrastructure—are notoriously difficult to measure, and using traditional benchmarks often just doesn't work. Several massive problems arise.

The first and biggest hurdle is the lack of investable indexes. As we discussed, a good benchmark should be investable. But how do you "invest" in the private equity market? You can't. These are private companies, not publicly traded stocks. The benchmarks that do exist are usually just databases that collect self-reported returns from a group of private equity or hedge funds. You can't buy this average; it's just a statistical creation. This makes it a weak baseline for comparison.

This leads directly to the second problem: these databases are plagued by survivorship bias. The indexes only include data from funds that have survived. The funds that performed terribly and went out of business are dropped from the history books. This makes the benchmark's historical performance look much better than it actually was, setting an artificially high bar for current managers. It's like judging a graduating class's potential by only looking at the valedictorians and ignoring everyone who dropped out.

Third, there's the issue of illiquidity and smoothed returns. A public stock has a price that changes every second. A private company or an office building might only be valued once a quarter or even once a year. This infrequent pricing makes their performance look incredibly smooth and stable over time. It masks the true underlying volatility. When you compare these "smoothed" returns to the volatile daily returns of a public market index, the alternative investment can look deceptively less risky. A manager might appear to be generating great risk-adjusted returns, but it's often just a statistical illusion caused by stale, infrequent pricing.

Finally, the very nature of many alternative investments is to be, well, alternative. A hedge fund might have a highly dynamic, secretive strategy that is designed to be completely different from any known market. How do you create a static benchmark for a strategy that is constantly evolving? It's like trying to judge a freeform jazz solo against a written musical score. The two are fundamentally different. For these unique strategies, finding a fair, appropriate, and investable benchmark can be next to impossible, leaving investors struggling to truly know how well their money is being managed.

The Analyst's Toolkit: Calculating and Interpreting Key Ratios

When we look beyond simple returns, we start to ask more intelligent questions. How did the manager achieve those returns? What risks did they take? And was it skill or just luck? These metrics help us answer those very questions.

1. The Sortino Ratio: Rewarding for Good Risk, Penalizing for Bad

The Sortino ratio is the thoughtful cousin of the more famous Sharpe ratio. While the Sharpe ratio penalizes all volatility (both up and down) equally, Sortino wisely argues that investors don't mind volatility that makes them money. Why would you penalize a stock for shooting up? Instead, the Sortino ratio focuses only on the harmful volatility—the kind that gives you sleepless nights.

Calculation:
The formula looks a bit like the Sharpe ratio, but with a crucial twist in the denominator.
Sortino Ratio=σdRp−Rf

Where:

Rp is the portfolio's actual or expected return.

Rf is the risk-free rate (like a T-bill).

σd is the downside deviation, or target semi-deviation. This is the magic ingredient; it only measures the volatility of returns that fall below a required minimum return.

Interpretation: A higher Sortino ratio is always better. It tells you that the investment manager is generating more return for each unit of "bad" risk they take on. If Manager A has a Sortino of 1.5 and Manager B has a Sortino of 0.8, it suggests Manager A is far more efficient at generating profits without exposing you to gut-wrenching drops. It's a measure of the quality of the return.

2. The Appraisal Ratio: Isolating Pure Skill

This ratio is all about measuring a manager's unique contribution. The market gives you a certain return (beta), but a truly skilled manager should be able to add something extra on top—that's their alpha. The Appraisal Ratio measures how much alpha the manager generates relative to the specific, non-market risks they took to get it.

Calculation:
Appraisal Ratio=$\sigma \epsilon a$

Where:

a (Alpha) is the excess return of the portfolio compared to its benchmark, after accounting for market risk. It's the manager's value-add.

$\sigma \epsilon$ (Sigma of Epsilon) is the unsystematic risk or tracking error. This is the volatility of the portfolio that can't be explained by the market's movements. It's the "manager-specific" risk.

Interpretation: A higher Appraisal Ratio suggests a more skilled manager. It shows they are not just generating alpha, but they are doing so consistently and efficiently, without a lot of erratic, unexplainable performance swings. Think of it as a measure of "alpha per unit of weirdness."

3. Upside/Downside Capture Ratios: Performance in Good Times and Bad

These ratios are wonderfully intuitive. They simply ask: When the market was up, how much of that gain did the manager capture? And when the market was down, how much of that loss did they suffer?

Calculation:
Upside Capture=Benchmark's Return in Up-Market PeriodsManager's Return in Up-Market Periods×100
Downside Capture=Benchmark's Return in Down-Market PeriodsManager's Return in Down-Market Periods×100

Interpretation:

For Upside Capture: You want a number greater than 100. An upside capture of 110% means that when the benchmark was up 10%, the manager was up 11%. They amplified the market's gains.

For Downside Capture: You want a number less than 100. A downside capture of 90% means that when the benchmark fell 10%, the manager only fell 9%. They provided a cushion during the storm. The ideal manager is like a well-designed boat: they catch the wind in full sail but are protected and stable in a tempest.

4. Maximum Drawdown & Drawdown Duration: Measuring the Pain

These two metrics work as a team to measure the worst-case scenario.

Maximum Drawdown (MDD): This is the single biggest percentage drop an investment has experienced from a peak to a subsequent trough. It's a gut check. It answers the question, "If my timing was absolutely terrible, what's the most I could have lost?" A lower MDD indicates better risk management.

Drawdown Duration: This measures how long the pain lasted. It's the total time from the start of the drawdown (the peak) until the investment recovered and reached that previous peak again. A shorter duration is obviously better. It tells you how resilient the strategy is and how quickly the manager can climb out of a hole. A massive drawdown that lasts for five years is far more psychologically damaging than one that recovers in six months.

Reading Between the Lines: Limitations of These Metrics

Numbers on a page can look definitive, but they are never the whole story. These powerful metrics, as useful as they are, come with important limitations that every savvy investor must understand. Relying on them blindly is like navigating a city using only a map from ten years ago; you'll miss all the new roads and roadblocks.

First and foremost is the "garbage in, garbage out" principle, especially regarding the choice of a benchmark. The Appraisal Ratio, alpha, and capture ratios are all relative to a benchmark. If a manager running a high-risk global tech fund is compared to a conservative bond index, their numbers will look heroic. But is that comparison fair or meaningful? No. An inappropriate benchmark can make a mediocre manager look like a genius or a skilled manager look inept. The benchmark must truly reflect the manager's stated investment style and universe.

Next, these metrics are incredibly sensitive to the time period you analyze. A manager who speciclized in growth stocks would have incredible Sortino and Appraisal ratios from 2015 to 2020. But if you shift that window to include a period like the 2022 downturn, their numbers might collapse. A short track record can be misleading. A manager might have one spectacular year that skews all their long-term averages. Skill is demonstrated through consistency across various market cycles—bull, bear, and everything in between—not just in a snapshot that happens to flatter their style.

Furthermore, these ratios tell you what happened, but they offer no insight into why. Did the manager achieve a low downside capture because of a repeatable, disciplined risk-management process? Or did they just get lucky by holding one stock that unexpectedly soared while everything else was crashing? The numbers can't distinguish between luck and skill. They don't reveal if a manager panicked and deviated from their strategy or if they stuck to their principles under pressure. The story behind the performance is just as crucial as the performance itself.

Another deep-seated issue lies within the models themselves. The Appraisal Ratio, for example, depends on alpha. Alpha is typically derived from models like the Capital Asset Pricing Model (CAPM), which have their own flaws and assumptions (like beta being a perfect measure of risk). If the underlying model for risk is flawed, the resulting measure of "skill" (alpha) will be flawed, too.

Finally, metrics can sometimes create perverse incentives. If a manager knows they are being judged heavily on, say, their Sortino ratio, they might be tempted to take on unusual risks that have a low probability of happening but would be catastrophic if they did (so-called "black swan" events). Their downside deviation might look great for years, right up until the moment it isn't. This is why a purely quantitative analysis is incomplete. It's a critical starting point, but it's not the finish line.

The Final Verdict: Evaluating the Skill of a Manager

So, how do we pull all this together to form a coherent judgment about an investment manager's skill? It's an exercise that is part science and part art. You must become an investigator, using the quantitative data as clues to build a qualitative case.

The first step is to look for consistency over time. Don't just look at the five-year number. Look at rolling three-year capture ratios, or the year-by-year Appraisal Ratio. Does the manager consistently protect capital in down years (low downside capture)? Do they consistently add value (positive alpha)? A manager who achieves an excellent result through a steady, repeatable process is almost certainly more skilled than one whose long-term average is propped up by a single, lucky home run.

Next, you must connect the numbers to the narrative. Every manager has a stated philosophy—"we are a deep value, contrarian fund," or "we focus on high-quality, defensive growth." The metrics should confirm this story. If the "defensive" manager has a high downside capture ratio (above 100%) and a terrifying maximum drawdown, then something is wrong. Either they aren't being truthful about their process, or they aren't very good at implementing it. This disconnect between words and numbers is a massive red flag.

The ultimate evaluation synthesizes these metrics into a complete profile. You aren't just looking for one good number. You're looking for a mosaic of data that paints a picture of a skilled operator. The dream manager profile would look something like this:

An Upside Capture Ratio comfortably over 100 and a Downside Capture Ratio well under 100. This demonstrates an ability to outperform in both bull and bear markets—the hallmark of tactical skill.

A high and consistent Sortino Ratio, indicating they generate strong returns without subjecting investors to painful losses. It shows they respect the downside.

A positive and stable Appraisal Ratio, proving their "alpha" is not a fluke but is generated efficiently and is a result of their unique process, not just market luck.

A manageable Maximum Drawdown and a reasonable Drawdown Duration. This shows that even when they are wrong, they don't blow up the portfolio and can recover relatively quickly.

In the end, evaluating a manager is about judging their decision-making process through the lens of performance data. The numbers are the evidence. A high return can be achieved by anyone who takes on enough risk or gets lucky. True skill lies in generating a pattern of superior risk-adjusted returns, consistently, across different market environments, in a way that aligns with a stated, disciplined process. That is the manager worth hiring.

Investment Manager Selection

The Intricate Dance of Manager Selection: A Deep Dive

Selecting the right investment manager is one of the most critical decisions an investor or an institution can make. It's a detailed process that goes far beyond simply looking at past performance. Think of it as hiring a crucial long-term partner for your financial journey. A robust selection process is methodical, disciplined, and multi-faceted, involving a deep investigation into both the numbers and the people behind them.

At its core, the process begins with a clear definition of what you're looking for. What is the specific role this manager will play in your portfolio? Are you seeking aggressive growth, steady income, or a hedge against volatility? This initial step, often called setting the mandate, shapes all subsequent decisions. Once the goals are clear, the search begins, often involving broad databases and industry networks to screen for potential candidates who fit the basic criteria.

This leads to the heart of the matter: due diligence. This isn't a single step but a comprehensive investigation broken into several key components. Quantitative due diligence is the numbers part. Here, you'll analyze historical returns, risk metrics (like standard deviation), and performance relative to a benchmark. But this is just the start. Qualitative due diligence is arguably more important. This involves understanding the firm's culture, its stability, and the alignment of its interests with yours. You'll investigate the investment team's experience, their tenure, and how they are compensated. Is their success tied to long-term performance, or are they incentivized to take short-term risks? Finally, operational due diligence ensures the manager has the infrastructure to protect your assets. This means examining their back-office operations, compliance procedures, trading systems, and disaster recovery plans. It's the less glamorous but absolutely essential part of ensuring your investment is in safe hands.

The Two Big Mistakes: Type I and Type II Errors

When it comes to hiring and firing investment managers, even the most thorough process can lead to mistakes. In the world of statistics and decision-making, these are categorized as Type I and Type II errors, and understanding them is crucial for long-term success.

A Type I error is the mistake of hiring or retaining a bad manager. Think of it as a "false positive." You reviewed a manager, their story was compelling, their recent numbers looked great, and you brought them on board. However, it turns out their success was due to luck, a single good call, or exposure to a risk you didn't fully appreciate. They go on to underperform, costing you money and opportunity. This is the more commonly discussed error because its consequences are often immediate and painful. Firing a manager who is genuinely skilled but going through a temporary rough patch is another form of a Type I error—letting go of a winner too soon.

On the other hand, a Type II error is the mistake of not hiring a good manager. This is a "false negative." You may have screened out a truly talented manager because their short-term track record was unimpressive, their strategy was unconventional, or their firm was new and small. You decided to pass, and that manager went on to produce stellar returns for years to come. The cost of a Type II error is an opportunity cost—the gains you missed out on. These errors are often harder to spot because you don't see the direct loss in your portfolio; you just see the success you could have had elsewhere. The fear of

making a Type I error (hiring a dud) often leads investors to be overly conservative, which in turn increases the chances of making a Type II error (passing on a gem). A truly effective selection process balances the risks of both. It requires the courage to look beyond the obvious and the discipline to avoid being swayed by short-term noise.
Looking Under the Hood: Returns-Based vs. Holdings-Based Analysis

How do you know if a manager is actually doing what they say they're doing? Two powerful techniques help answer this question: returns-based and holdings-based style analysis. They are like two different ways of diagnosing a car engine—one listens to the sound it makes, while the other involves taking it apart to see the individual components.

Returns-based style analysis is the "listening" approach. It uses a manager's historical returns and statistically compares them to the returns of various market indexes (like large-cap growth stocks, small-cap value stocks, international bonds, etc.). The goal is to determine which combination of these indexes best explains the manager's performance. For example, the analysis might reveal that a manager who claims to be a "go-anywhere" stock picker actually generates returns that look 80% like the S&P 500 and 20% like a small-cap index. This can be very useful for quickly assessing a manager's "style drift"—are they sticking to their stated strategy? It's relatively easy and inexpensive to perform, as it only requires the manager's return history.

Holdings-based style analysis, conversely, is the "take it apart" approach. It involves looking directly at the individual securities the manager owns at a specific point in time. By analyzing the characteristics of each stock or bond in the portfolio—such as its market capitalization, price-to-earnings ratio, dividend yield, and industry sector—you can get a very precise, bottom-up picture of the manager's investment style. This method provides a much more detailed and accurate snapshot than returns-based analysis. It can reveal specific concentrations or risks that might otherwise be hidden. The downside is that it requires full portfolio transparency from the manager, which not all are willing to provide, and the analysis is only as good as the moment in time the data was captured. A manager could change their portfolio the very next day. Using both methods together provides the most complete picture of a manager's true investment style.

Measuring the Bumps in the Road: Key Risk and Performance Metrics

Past performance is never a guarantee of future results, but analyzing how a manager achieved their returns can tell you a lot about their process and the risks they take. Several key metrics help paint this picture, moving beyond simple average returns to evaluate the manager's performance during different market conditions.

The upside capture ratio and downside capture ratio are fantastic tools for this. The upside capture tells you what percentage of the market's gains the manager "captured" during months when the market went up. A ratio over 100% means they outperformed in up markets. The downside capture shows what percentage of the market's losses they experienced in months when the market went down. Here, a ratio below 100% is desirable, as it means they protected capital better than the market. A manager who captures 110% of the upside but only 80% of the downside is demonstrating a very attractive, asymmetric return profile.

Maximum drawdown is another critical, gut-check metric. It measures the largest single peak-to-trough drop a portfolio has experienced. This number tells you the most pain an investor would have endured by investing with that manager. A smaller maximum drawdown suggests better risk management. Closely related is the drawdown duration, which measures how long it took for the portfolio to recover from that loss and get back to its previous peak. A long drawdown duration can be psychologically taxing for investors and can indicate a strategy that struggles to rebound. Together, these metrics help you understand not just the potential rewards, but also the potential pain and the time it might take to heal from it. They provide a realistic view of the journey you might expect with a particular manager.

The Core of It All: Philosophy and Process

Beyond all the numbers and metrics lies the most fundamental aspect of a manager evaluation: their investment philosophy and decision-making process. This is the bedrock upon which everything else is built. A clearly articulated philosophy acts as a compass, guiding all investment decisions, especially during times of market stress.

An investment philosophy is the manager's core belief about how markets work and where investment opportunities come from. Are they a deep-value investor who believes the market overreacts to bad news, allowing them to buy good companies at cheap prices? Are they a growth investor who believes in identifying innovative companies that will define the future? Or are they a quantitative manager who believes models and algorithms can exploit market inefficiencies? There is no single "right" philosophy, but it must be consistent, sensible, and have been tested over time. You need to understand it and, just as importantly, believe in it yourself.

The investment process is the practical application of that philosophy. It's the "how." It should be a structured, repeatable, and disciplined framework for turning the philosophy into a portfolio. Key questions to ask include: How do they generate new ideas? What research do they conduct before making an investment? Who makes the final decision—a single star manager or a committee? How do they construct the portfolio and manage risk? And, crucially, what is their sell discipline? Knowing when to sell an investment is just as important as knowing when to buy. A manager with a well-defined and consistently applied process is far more likely to generate sustainable long-term results than one who relies on gut feel or is constantly changing their approach. Ultimately, you are investing in this philosophy and process, trusting that the people in charge have the skill and discipline to execute it successfully through all market cycles.

The Human Element: How Behavior Shapes Investment Decisions

We like to think that investing is a purely logical process, driven by data and rigorous analysis. The reality is that investment decisions are made by humans, and humans are susceptible to a wide range of behavioral biases. These psychological shortcuts and emotional responses can have a significant impact on an investment team's performance, often leading to suboptimal outcomes. Understanding these factors is the first step toward building a more robust investment process.

One of the most common biases is overconfidence. Investment professionals are smart, successful people, and it's easy for them to believe they know more than they actually do. This can lead to taking on excessive risk, failing to adequately diversify, or holding onto losing positions for too long, convinced that they will eventually be proven right. A related issue is the illusion of control, where a team might believe they can influence market outcomes that are, in reality, far beyond their control.

Another powerful bias is herding. The financial world can feel like a very small place, and the pressure to conform is immense. When everyone seems to be buying a particular stock or investing in a certain sector, it's incredibly difficult to be the one who stands apart. This can lead to investment bubbles, where asset prices become detached from their fundamental value, only to come crashing down later. The fear of missing out (FOMO) is a powerful motivator, and it can cause even the most disciplined teams to abandon their long-term strategy in favor of chasing short-term trends.

Confirmation bias is the tendency to seek out and interpret information that confirms our existing beliefs, while ignoring evidence that contradicts them. For an investment team, this can mean that once they've made a decision to invest in a company, they will subconsciously filter news and data to support that decision. This can create a dangerous echo chamber, preventing the team from objectively reassessing their positions and cutting their losses when necessary.

So, how can these behavioral pitfalls be mitigated? One of the most effective techniques is to foster a culture of psychological safety and intellectual honesty. Team members must feel comfortable challenging the consensus view without fear of ridicule or retribution. Designating a "devil's advocate" for major decisions can be a formal way to ensure that dissenting opinions are heard and considered.

Developing and adhering to a structured decision-making process is also crucial. This means having a clear, written investment philosophy and a repeatable process for researching, debating, and making investment decisions. Using checklists can help ensure that all relevant factors are considered and can act as a circuit breaker against emotional, impulsive choices.

Finally, conducting regular pre-mortems and post-mortems can be invaluable. In a pre-mortem, the team imagines that an investment has failed and works backward to identify all the things that could have gone wrong. This helps to surface potential risks that might have been overlooked. A post-mortem, on the other hand, is a review of past decisions—both good and bad—to learn from mistakes and institutionalize successes. By creating a formal process for reflection, teams can become more self-aware and less susceptible to the same old behavioral traps.

Structure Matters: Pooled Vehicles vs. Separate Accounts

Once you have a sense of the people, you need to consider the structure in which they operate. Investment managers typically offer their strategies through two main structures: pooled investment vehicles and separate accounts. Each has its own set of costs and benefits, and the right choice will depend on the specific needs and circumstances of the investor.

Pooled investment vehicles, such as mutual funds, exchange-traded funds (ETFs), and hedge funds, do exactly what their name implies: they pool the assets of multiple investors into a single fund. This fund then owns a portfolio of securities, and each investor owns shares or units of the fund, representing their pro-rata claim on the underlying assets.

The primary benefit of pooled vehicles is economies of scale. By pooling assets, investors can access professional management and a diversified portfolio for a much lower investment than would be required to build a similar portfolio on their own. The operational and trading costs are spread across a larger asset base, which generally translates into lower fees for the end investor. Pooled funds also offer simplicity. The fund manager handles all the trading, record-keeping, and administration, making it a relatively hands-off experience for the investor.

However, this simplicity comes with a lack of control and transparency. Investors in a pooled fund do not own the underlying securities directly; they own shares of the fund. They have no say in the specific investment decisions being made. Furthermore, the activities of other investors in the fund can affect you. For example, if many investors decide to redeem their shares at once, the fund manager may be forced to sell securities at an inopportune time to raise cash, potentially creating a tax liability for the remaining investors.

Separate accounts, on the other hand, offer a much higher degree of customization and control. In this arrangement, an investment manager is hired to manage a portfolio of securities exclusively for a single client. The assets are held in an account in the client's name, and the client directly owns the underlying securities.

The biggest advantage of a separate account is customization. The portfolio can be tailored to the client's specific risk tolerance, time horizon, and ethical or social considerations. For example, a client might instruct the manager to avoid investing in certain industries, like tobacco or fossil fuels. Separate accounts also offer greater tax efficiency. Because the client owns the securities directly, the manager can engage in tax-loss harvesting—selling losing positions to offset gains elsewhere in the portfolio—which is not possible in a pooled fund structure.

The main drawback of separate accounts is cost. Because they do not benefit from economies of scale, the management fees are typically higher. There are also usually higher minimum investment requirements, putting them out of reach for many smaller investors. They also require more hands-on involvement from the client, who will need to review and approve the investment policy statement and stay engaged with the manager on an ongoing basis.

Ultimately, the choice between a pooled vehicle and a separate account involves a trade-off between cost and control. For many investors, the simplicity and lower costs of pooled funds make them the more practical option. For wealthier investors with more complex needs, the customization and tax benefits of a separate account may be well worth the higher price tag.

The Fine Print: Understanding Manager Contracts

The investment management contract is the legal document that governs the relationship between you and your investment manager. It's often long, filled with legal jargon, and easy to overlook. But reading and understanding this document is absolutely essential, as it outlines the rights, responsibilities, and obligations of both parties.

The contract will typically begin with a section on the appointment of the manager. This provision formally grants the manager the authority to make investment decisions on your behalf, subject to the constraints laid out in the investment guidelines. These guidelines are one of the most important parts of the contract. They define the investment universe (what the manager can and cannot invest in), the strategic asset allocation, and any specific restrictions you wish to impose. This is where you would specify any ethical or social screens you want applied to your portfolio.

The duties and responsibilities of the manager will also be detailed. This includes their obligation to act as a fiduciary—meaning they must act in your best interest—and to exercise a certain standard of care in their decision-making. The contract will also specify the services the manager will provide, such as portfolio management, performance reporting, and custody of assets.

Of course, the contract will also spell out the fees you will be paying. This is an area that requires close scrutiny. Fees can be structured in many different ways, and it's important to understand exactly how they are calculated and when they will be charged. We'll delve deeper into performance-based fees in a moment, but even a simple asset-based fee can have nuances, such as whether it's charged in advance or in arrears, and how the value of your assets is calculated for billing purposes.

Other important provisions include the term and termination of the contract. This section will specify the initial term of the agreement and the conditions under which either party can terminate it. Pay close attention to any notice periods or potential termination fees. The contract will also include clauses on confidentiality, liability, and indemnification. The liability clause, in particular, is critical, as it defines the circumstances under which the manager can be held responsible for investment losses.

The primary advantage of a well-drafted contract is clarity. It ensures that both you and the manager are on the same page regarding the scope of the engagement, the investment strategy, and the fees. This can help to prevent misunderstandings and disputes down the road. The main disadvantage is that these contracts are often drafted by the manager's lawyers and can be heavily weighted in their favor. It is always a good idea to have your own legal counsel review the document before you sign it. Don't be afraid to negotiate. Key terms, especially fees and investment guidelines, can often be adjusted to better suit your needs.

Paying for Performance: Three Types of Fees

While many managers charge a simple fee based on a percentage of assets under management, it is increasingly common to see performance-based fees. The idea is simple: to better align the interests of the manager with the interests of the client. If the client does well, the manager does well. There are three basic forms this can take.

The most straightforward is a fee based on a share of the profits. For example, a hedge fund might charge "2 and 20," which means a 2% management fee on total assets, plus a 20% performance fee on any profits generated. This structure is highly motivating for the manager, as their potential upside is significant. However, it can also create a perverse incentive to take on excessive risk. Since the manager shares in the gains but not the losses, they might be tempted to make big bets in the hope of generating a large fee, even if those bets have a low probability of success.

To mitigate this, many performance fee structures include a high-water mark. This means that the manager is only entitled to a performance fee on new profits. If the portfolio value drops, the manager will not earn another performance fee until the portfolio has recovered to its previous high point. This prevents the manager from getting paid multiple times for simply recovering lost ground.

A second type of performance-based fee is one that is symmetric around a benchmark. In this structure, the manager's fee is adjusted up or down based on their performance relative to a pre-agreed-upon benchmark index, like the S&P 500. If the manager outperforms the benchmark, their fee increases. If they underperform, their fee is reduced. This is a fairer structure, as it rewards the manager for their skill (or "alpha") rather than for simply riding a rising market. It also means the manager has some skin in the game on the downside; underperformance will directly impact their compensation.

The third form is a bonus based on outperformance, with a cap. This is similar to the symmetric fee, but the upside is limited. For example, the manager might earn a bonus for outperforming their benchmark by up to 5%, but any outperformance beyond that does not result in a higher fee. This can be a good way to motivate the manager without encouraging them to swing for the fences. It recognizes that extreme outperformance is often the result of luck rather than skill, and it helps to keep the manager focused on their core strategy.

Each of these structures has its pros and cons. The key is to find a structure that fairly compensates the manager for their skill while also creating the right incentives. A good performance fee structure should reward outperformance, but not at the expense of prudent risk management.

Deciphering the Schedule: Analyzing a Performance Fee

Reading a performance-based fee schedule can be intimidating, but it's a crucial skill for any serious investor.

Let's break down how to analyze a sample schedule to understand what you're really paying for.

Imagine a fee schedule that looks something like this:

Base Fee: 0.75% on all assets under management.

Benchmark: S&P 500 Total Return Index.

Performance Adjustment: +/- 0.05% for every 1% of outperformance or underperformance relative to the benchmark.

Performance Measurement Period: Rolling 36 months.

Maximum Fee: 1.25%.

Minimum Fee: 0.25%.

The first thing to look at is the base fee. This is what you'll pay regardless of performance. At 0.75%, this is a fairly standard fee for an actively managed account.

Next, look at the benchmark. Is it appropriate for the manager's strategy? In this case, the S&P 500 is a good benchmark for a U.S. large-cap equity manager. If the manager were investing in international small-cap stocks, this would be an inappropriate benchmark, and it would be easy for them to "outperform" it simply by taking on more risk.

The core of the schedule is the performance adjustment. Here, the fee is adjusted up or down by 0.05% for every 1% of performance relative to the benchmark. This is a symmetric structure, which is good. It means the manager is penalized for underperformance as well as rewarded for outperformance.

Let's run a scenario. Suppose over the last 36 months, the manager's portfolio returned 12% per year, and the S&P 500 returned 10% per year. The manager has outperformed by 2% per year. The performance adjustment would be 2 * 0.05% = 0.10%. So, the total fee would be the base fee of 0.75% plus the performance adjustment of 0.10%, for a total of 0.85%.

Now, let's say the manager underperformed, returning 8% while the benchmark returned 10%. They underperformed by 2%. The fee adjustment would be a reduction of 0.10%. The total fee would be 0.75% - 0.10% = 0.65%.

The performance measurement period is also critical. A rolling 36-month period is good because it evaluates performance over a longer time frame, which helps to smooth out short-term market noise and gives a better picture of the manager's skill. A shorter period, like one year, could encourage the manager to take on a lot of risk in an attempt to hit a short-term home run.

Finally, look at the cap and floor on the fee. A maximum fee of 1.25% and a minimum of 0.25% seems reasonable. The cap prevents the manager from earning an astronomical fee in a year of extreme outperformance (which could be due to luck), and the floor ensures that they still get paid something for their work, even if they underperform.

By carefully analyzing each component of the fee schedule, you can get a much clearer picture of how your manager will be compensated and what incentives that compensation structure creates. It's a vital step in ensuring that your interests and your manager's interests are truly aligned.

Overview of the Global Investment Performance Standards

Objectives, Scope, and Benefits of GIPS

The Global Investment Performance Standards, or GIPS, represent a universal set of ethical principles designed to standardize how investment firms calculate and present their performance results to clients. Think of it as a common language for investment performance. The main goal is to ensure that the information prospective clients see is both fair and directly comparable across different managers. This transparency is at the heart of GIPS. The standards are voluntary, but they have become the gold standard in the investment world, adopted by firms in dozens of countries.

The scope of GIPS is quite broad. It applies to any investment firm that wants to claim compliance and market its services to a global audience. The standards cover all aspects of performance reporting, from how data is collected to how it's presented in marketing materials. For clients and investors, the benefits are immense. It instills confidence and trust, knowing that the performance numbers haven't been cherry-picked or manipulated. It allows for true "apples-to-apples" comparisons, making it easier to select the right investment manager. For the managers themselves, adopting GIPS levels the playing field, enhances their credibility, and often strengthens their internal processes and controls. It's a powerful statement about their commitment to ethical practices.

Fundamentals of GIPS Compliance

Achieving compliance with GIPS is a serious commitment for an investment firm. The first fundamental step is defining the "firm" itself. This isn't just a legal definition; for GIPS purposes, the firm is the distinct investment management entity that is held out to clients as a specific business. It could be a whole corporation, a subsidiary, or a specific division, but it must be clearly defined. This definition is crucial because GIPS compliance is a firm-wide endeavor. You can't just pick and choose which parts of your business will comply; it's all or nothing for the defined entity.

Another core concept is the firm's definition of "discretion." This refers to the level of independent control a portfolio manager has over the investment decisions for a particular portfolio. A firm must establish a clear, written policy that defines what it means for a portfolio to be discretionary. This is vital because only discretionary portfolios are typically included in a firm's performance composites. If a client, for instance, places significant restrictions on an account, like prohibiting investment in certain sectors, that portfolio might be deemed non-discretionary and excluded. The key is that the definition must be applied consistently to all portfolios.

Return Calculation Methodologies

GIPS sets strict rules for calculating returns to ensure uniformity. A cornerstone of this is the requirement to use time-weighted rates of return, which neutralize the impact of cash flows. This is critical. Imagine a client adds a large sum of money to their account right before the market goes up. A simple return calculation would look inflated, but a time-weighted return shows the manager's actual performance, independent of that client's decision. GIPS mandates that portfolios must be valued at least monthly, and for periods starting on or after January 1, 2010, firms must value them whenever there are large external cash flows.

The treatment of fees and expenses is also standardized. Returns must be calculated after deducting the actual trading expenses incurred. When it comes to reporting, firms are required to show their performance both gross-of-fees (before deducting management fees) and net-of-fees (after deducting management fees). This gives clients a clear picture of both the manager's skill and the actual return they would have received. As for cash, if a manager has discretion over the cash holdings within a portfolio, that cash must be included in the return calculations. It's all part of the portfolio's total assets.

The GIPS Valuation Hierarchy

Accurate asset valuation is the foundation of credible performance reporting. To ensure consistency, GIPS recommends a specific valuation hierarchy. This is a framework that prioritizes the use of the most objective and verifiable pricing sources available. The ideal, and top of the hierarchy, is to use fair market values based on observable market prices from an active market. Think of the closing price of a publicly traded stock on a major exchange—it's clear, objective, and easily verified.

When direct market prices aren't available, firms must move down the hierarchy. The next best option might be prices for similar assets in active markets or prices for identical assets in markets that are not very active. If those aren't available, the firm might rely on other observable inputs, like interest rates or yield curves. At the very bottom of the hierarchy are unobservable inputs, which require the firm to use its own assumptions and models to estimate a value. While sometimes necessary for illiquid or private assets, GIPS requires that firms have clear, documented policies for these situations to ensure the valuations are as fair and consistent as possible.

Composite Return Calculations

A composite is an aggregation of individual portfolios into a single group that represents a specific investment strategy or objective. For instance, a firm might have a "U.S. Large-Cap Growth" composite. GIPS requires that composite returns be calculated by asset-weighting the individual portfolio returns within that composite. This means that larger portfolios have a proportionally greater impact on the composite's overall return.

There are different methods to do this, but a common one is to weight each portfolio's return by its beginning-of-period market value. Alternatively, a firm could weight portfolios by their beginning market value plus a weighted average of their cash flows during the period. Whatever method the firm chooses, it must be applied consistently across all of its composites. This asset-weighting principle is crucial because it ensures the composite return accurately reflects the performance of the entire strategy, preventing a small, stellar-performing portfolio from skewing the results of the group.

The Meaning of "Discretionary" in Composites

In the context of GIPS, "discretionary" is a critical gatekeeper for composite construction. It essentially means the investment manager has the primary authority to make investment decisions for the portfolio. The portfolio must be managed according to the intended strategy of the composite it would belong to. If a portfolio's mandate is so constrained by the client that the manager cannot fully implement their strategy, it would likely be considered non-discretionary.

For example, imagine a manager runs a global equity strategy. A client wants to invest but insists that no more than 10% of the portfolio can be invested outside of North

America. If the manager's strategy normally involves a 30% allocation to European and Asian markets, this restriction is significant. It prevents the manager from managing the portfolio in line with the strategy's goals. Therefore, the firm would likely classify this portfolio as non-discretionary and exclude it from the global equity composite. A firm's written definition of discretion is the ultimate guide, and its consistent application is key to GIPS compliance.

Role of Mandates in Composite Construction

Investment mandates, objectives, and strategies are the building blocks of composites. Each composite must be defined according to a specific investment approach. The goal is to group together all portfolios that are managed with the same distinct style. For instance, a firm can't just create a generic "Equity" composite. It needs to be more specific, like "U.S. Small-Cap Value" or "Emerging Markets Debt."

The mandate given by the client for a specific portfolio determines which, if any, composite it should be placed in. If a portfolio's investment mandate aligns with the strategy of an existing composite, and it's discretionary, it must be included in that composite. This rule is designed to prevent firms from cherry-picking their best-performing accounts. The definition of each composite must be clear and consistently applied, ensuring that when a potential client looks at a composite's performance, they are seeing a representation of all portfolios managed under that specific strategy.

Requirements for Composite Construction

GIPS has strict rules about how and when portfolios enter and leave composites to maintain the integrity of the performance record. First, all actual, fee-paying, discretionary portfolios must be included in at least one composite. A new portfolio must be added to its appropriate composite in a timely manner, typically at the beginning of the next full performance period (e.g., the next month or quarter) after the portfolio comes under management.

When a portfolio is terminated, it must be included in the composite's historical performance up to the last full measurement period it was under management. You can't just remove a poorly performing portfolio from history as if it never existed. Similarly, switching portfolios between composites is heavily scrutinized. It should only be done if the client's mandate changes, and the switch must be documented. These rules prevent firms from manipulating composite performance by strategically moving accounts around.

Presentation and Reporting Requirements

When a GIPS-compliant firm presents its performance, it must follow a standardized format. This is what's known as a GIPS Report. The report must include a wealth of information to give clients a full and fair picture. For each composite, the firm must show at least five years of GIPS-compliant performance history, or performance since the composite's inception if it's younger than five years. After presenting five years, the firm must add another year of performance each year, up to a minimum of ten years.

The report must also include key statistics, such as the composite's annual return for each year, the number of portfolios in the composite, the amount of assets in the composite, and a measure of the dispersion of returns within the composite (like the standard deviation). Furthermore, the firm must disclose important information, including a description of the composite strategy, the fee schedule, and the specific GIPS compliance statement. This level of required disclosure ensures that clients have all the necessary context to understand the performance numbers they are seeing.

Linking Performance of a Past Firm

Sometimes, a team of portfolio managers might leave one firm to start a new one, or a firm might be acquired. GIPS has specific provisions that allow the historical performance record to move with them, but only under strict conditions. The primary condition is that substantially all the decision-makers who were responsible for that track record must be employed at the new firm. It can't just be one junior member of the team.

Additionally, the staff and the decision-making process at the new firm must remain substantially the same as they were at the old firm. The goal is to ensure that the historical record is truly representative of the team and strategy being offered at the new firm. The new firm must also have records that document and support the historical performance being claimed. When this performance is presented, it must be clearly disclosed that the results came from a prior firm. This allows for portability of a track record while maintaining transparency for potential clients.

The Purpose and Process of Verification

Verification is the process of having an independent third party—a verifier—conduct tests on a firm to confirm that it has complied with all the firm-wide GIPS requirements. While claiming GIPS compliance is voluntary, verification is highly recommended as it adds another layer of credibility. The purpose of verification is not to audit the performance of a specific composite, but rather to confirm that the firm has designed its policies and procedures to be in line with the GIPS standards and has applied them consistently.

The process involves the verifier reviewing the firm's policies on things like the definition of the firm, discretion, composite construction, and data valuation. They will sample portfolios to ensure these policies are being followed correctly. If the firm passes, it can state that it has been "verified by [Name of Verifier]." This verification provides prospective clients with a significant level of assurance that the firm's claim of GIPS compliance is robust and that its performance presentations are ethically constructed and reliable.

Chapter 4: Derivatives and Risk Management

Options Strategies

A Guide to Options Strategies: From Basics to Advanced Concepts

Options trading can seem like a complex world filled with jargon and intricate strategies. However, at its core, it's about using contracts that give you the right, but not the obligation, to buy or sell an underlying asset at a specific price. This guide will walk you through some fundamental and more advanced options strategies, breaking them down into simple, understandable concepts.
Replicating Asset Returns with Options

Did you know you can mimic the experience of owning a stock without actually buying it? This is one of the fascinating aspects of options, made possible through a principle called put-call parity. Imagine you want the same financial outcome as holding 100 shares of a company, say XYZ Corp. Instead of buying the shares directly, you could buy a call option and sell a put option.

The call option gives you the right to buy XYZ at a set price (the strike price), so if the stock price soars, your call option becomes valuable, just as if you owned the stock. On the other hand, selling a put option obligates you to buy the stock if the price drops. This mirrors the downside risk of owning the stock. By combining these two positions with a risk-free investment like a government bond, you can create a "synthetic" long stock position. The profit and loss profile of this options combo will be nearly identical to that of owning the stock outright. This powerful concept shows just how versatile options can be, allowing you to create customized risk and return profiles that suit your specific market views.

The Covered Call: Generating Income from Your Holdings

A covered call is a popular strategy for investors who already own an underlying asset, like a stock, and are looking to generate some extra income from it. The goal here isn't necessarily to hit a home run but to consistently earn a premium.

Investment Objective: The primary objective is to generate income from the premiums received by selling call options. It's for investors who are neutral to slightly bullish on their stock in the short term. They believe the stock won't rise significantly before the option expires.

Structure: You own at least 100 shares of a stock and sell one call option for every 100 shares you own. This is why it's called "covered"—your stock ownership covers the obligation of the call option you sold.

Payoff and Value at Expiration: If the stock price at expiration is below the strike price, the option expires worthless, and you keep the premium. Your stock is untouched. If the stock price is above the strike price, the buyer will likely exercise the option, and you'll have to sell your shares at the strike price.

Profit and Risks: Your maximum profit is the premium you received plus any capital gains up to the strike price. The biggest risk is that the stock price skyrockets. You'll miss out on those significant gains because you're obligated to sell at the lower strike price. Your maximum loss is the price you paid for the stock minus the premium received, which would happen if the stock price went to zero.

Breakeven Price: Your breakeven point is the purchase price of your stock minus the premium you received for selling the call.

The Protective Put: Insurance for Your Portfolio

Think of a protective put as an insurance policy for your stocks. If you're worried about a potential downturn but don't want to sell your shares, a protective put can offer you peace of mind.

Investment Objective: The main goal is to protect against a decline in the price of a stock you own. It's for investors who are long-term bullish but short-term bearish or simply want to hedge their downside risk.

Structure: You own at least 100 shares of a stock and buy one put option for every 100 shares.

Payoff and Value at Expiration: If the stock price at expiration is above the strike price, the put option expires worthless, and you lose the premium you paid. However, if the stock price drops below the strike price, your put option becomes valuable, offsetting the losses in your stock.

Profit and Risks: Your maximum profit is theoretically unlimited, as the stock price can rise indefinitely (minus the cost of the put). Your maximum loss is limited to the premium you paid for the put option plus the difference between the stock price and the strike price. The risk is that the stock price doesn't fall, and you lose the premium you paid for the "insurance."

Breakeven Price: The breakeven point is the purchase price of your stock plus the premium you paid for the put.

Comparing Deltas: Covered Calls, Protective Puts, and Long Stock

Delta is a measure of how much an option's price is expected to change for every $1 move in the underlying stock. A long stock position has a delta of 1. A short forward position has a delta of -1.

A covered call position has a delta of less than 1. You start with the stock's delta of 1, but by selling a call option (which has a positive delta), you are effectively reducing your overall delta. This means your position won't gain as much as a simple long stock position when the stock price rises.

A protective put position also has a delta of less than 1 but for a different reason. The long stock has a delta of 1, and you add a long put, which has a negative delta. This combination reduces the overall delta, providing a buffer if the stock price falls.

Buying a Call vs. Selling a Put on a Short Position

If you've shorted a stock, you're betting its price will go down. Buying a call option can act as a form of insurance. If the stock price unexpectedly rises, your losses on the short position can be unlimited. However, the call option will increase in value, offsetting some of those losses. Selling a put on a short position is a more aggressive strategy. You're still betting the stock will go down, but you're also collecting a premium from the put. This increases your potential profit if you're right, but it doesn't offer the same protection as buying a call if the stock price rises.

More Advanced Strategies: Spreads, Straddles, and Collars

Bull Spread: This strategy is for when you're moderately bullish on a stock. You buy a call option at a certain strike price and sell another call option with a higher strike price but the same expiration date. This limits your potential profit but also reduces the cost of the position. Your maximum profit is the difference between the strike prices minus the net premium paid. Your maximum loss is the net premium paid.

Bear Spread: The opposite of a bull spread, this is for when you're moderately bearish. You buy a put option at a certain strike price and sell another put option with a lower strike price and the same expiration. This limits your profit if the stock falls but also reduces your cost.

Straddle: A straddle is a bet on volatility. You buy both a call and a put option with the same strike price and expiration date. You're not betting on the direction of the stock, just that it will make a big move, either up or down. Your profit is potentially unlimited, but your maximum loss is the total premium you paid for both options.

Collar: A collar is a way to protect gains in a stock you own. You buy a protective put to limit your downside and sell a covered call to finance the cost of the put. This creates a "collar" around your stock's price, limiting both your potential gains and losses.

Calendar Spreads: A Play on Time

A calendar spread involves buying and selling options of the same type (both calls or both puts) and the same strike price but with different expiration dates. You might sell a short-term option and buy a longer-term one. This strategy profits from the passage of time and changes in implied volatility. The idea is that the shorter-term option will lose value faster than the longer-term one.

Volatility Skew and Smile: The Nuances of Option Pricing:
In a perfect world, the implied volatility of options would be the same across all strike prices. But in reality, it's not. A "volatility smile" occurs when options that are far out-of-the-money or in-the-money have higher implied volatility than at-the-money options. A "volatility skew" is more common in equity markets, where out-of-the-money puts have higher implied volatility than out-of-the-money calls. This reflects the market's fear of a crash being greater than its hope for a rally.

Choosing the Right Strategy:
The best option strategy depends entirely on your investment objectives and your outlook on the market.

If you're bullish, you might consider buying calls or using a bull spread.

If you're bearish, buying puts or using a bear spread could be appropriate.

If you expect low volatility, a covered call might be a good choice.

If you anticipate a big price swing but are unsure of the direction, a straddle could be the way to go.

Using Options for Targeted Equity Risk Exposure
Options are incredibly powerful tools for managing risk. If you want to reduce your exposure to a particular stock or sector without selling your holdings, you can buy put options. Conversely, if you want to increase your exposure to a potential upside move, you can buy call options. This allows you to fine-tune your portfolio's risk profile with a level of precision that's difficult to achieve with stocks and bonds alone. By understanding these strategies, you can begin to unlock the full potential of options in your investment journey.

Swaps, Forwards, and Futures Strategies

Mastering Portfolio Strategy: A Guide to Swaps, Forwards, and Futures

Navigating the world of investments can feel like steering a ship through ever-changing seas. Market conditions shift, risks emerge, and opportunities appear and vanish in the blink of an eye. For portfolio managers, the key to success isn't just picking the right stocks or bonds; it's about having the right tools to skillfully manage the journey. Among the most powerful of these tools are derivatives—financial contracts whose value is derived from an underlying asset.

While they can sound intimidating, instruments like swaps, forwards, and futures are essentially strategic agreements that allow investors to fine-tune their portfolios. They can be used defensively to protect against losses or offensively to capture gains. Think of them not as complex gambles, but as precision instruments for shaping a portfolio's risk and return profile. This guide will break down how these derivatives work across interest rates, currencies, and equities, making these sophisticated concepts easy to grasp.

Modifying Portfolio Risk with Interest Rate Derivatives

Imagine you manage a portfolio heavily invested in fixed-rate bonds. Your biggest fear is rising interest rates, which would cause the value of your bonds to fall. This is where an interest rate swap becomes your best friend. A swap is an agreement between two parties to exchange cash flows over a specific period. In this case, you could enter into a "plain vanilla" interest rate swap where you agree to pay a fixed interest rate to a counterparty in exchange for receiving a floating rate from them.

If interest rates rise, the floating rate you receive goes up, offsetting the losses on your bond portfolio. You've effectively transformed your fixed-rate exposure into a floating-rate one, protecting your capital. This is a classic hedging strategy.

Conversely, what if you expect interest rates to fall? You could use a swap to do the opposite—pay a floating rate and receive a fixed rate. If you're right and rates decline, the floating payments you owe will decrease while you continue to receive the steady, higher fixed payment, generating a positive return.

Forwards and futures achieve similar goals but in slightly different ways. A Forward Rate Agreement (FRA) lets you lock in an interest rate for a future period. For instance, if you need to borrow money in three months but fear rates will rise, you can use an FRA to fix your borrowing cost today. An interest rate future, which is a standardized, exchange-traded contract, can be used to speculate on the direction of rates or to hedge a portfolio with remarkable precision. By selling futures, you protect against rising rates; by buying them, you bet on falling rates. These tools give you the power to sculpt your portfolio's sensitivity to interest rate movements.

Navigating Global Markets with Currency Derivatives

In today's interconnected world, many portfolios have international exposure, which introduces currency risk. Let's say you own shares in a successful Japanese company. The stock performs well in yen, but if the yen weakens against your home currency, your returns could be wiped out when you convert the money back.

This is where currency forwards come in handy. A forward is a private contract to buy or sell a currency at a predetermined exchange rate on a specific future date.

To hedge your Japanese investment, you could enter into a forward contract to sell yen and buy your home currency at today's rate. Now, even if the yen's value falls, you've already locked in your exchange rate, protecting your profits. You've removed the currency uncertainty from the equation.

Currency futures work just like forwards but are traded on an exchange, making them more standardized and accessible. If you anticipated the euro would strengthen against the U.S. dollar, you could buy euro futures. If your prediction comes true, the value of your futures contract will rise, and you can sell it for a profit, all without ever holding the physical currency.

A currency swap takes this a step further, involving the exchange of both principal and interest payments in different currencies. A U.S. company operating in Europe, for example, might issue debt in euros and then swap those euro-denominated payments with a European company that needs U.S. dollars. This allows both firms to borrow in their desired currency more cheaply, effectively managing long-term foreign exchange risk and improving their return on international projects.

Shaping Equity Exposure with Derivatives

Equity derivatives offer an incredibly flexible and capital-efficient way to manage a stock portfolio. Suppose you want to gain exposure to the S&P 500 index but don't want to buy all 500 individual stocks. You could simply buy S&P 500 futures contracts. This gives you the performance of the index with a much smaller initial cash outlay. If the market goes up, your futures position becomes profitable, mirroring the return you would have gotten from holding the stocks. This is a powerful way to quickly and cheaply adjust your portfolio's market exposure.

What if you hold a large, undiversified portfolio of a single stock and are worried about a short-term downturn but don't want to sell the shares? An equity swap provides a clever solution. You can enter into a swap where you agree to pay the total return of your stock to a counterparty (like a bank) and, in return, receive a steady floating interest rate (like LIBOR) or the return of a diversified index. For the duration of the swap, you've essentially traded away the risk of your single stock in favor of a more stable return, all without triggering a taxable event by selling your shares.

Equity forwards and options can also be used for tactical moves. An investor might use a forward contract to lock in the purchase price of a stock they want to buy in the future. Options give the holder the right, but not the obligation, to buy or sell a stock at a certain price, offering a way to bet on short-term price movements or protect a portfolio from a market crash. These derivatives allow managers to fine-tune their equity risk with surgical precision.

Understanding Volatility and Variance Swaps

Beyond direction, sophisticated investors also manage a portfolio's exposure to volatility—the magnitude of market swings. Volatility derivatives allow you to trade this risk directly. The most common tool is a derivative based on the Cboe Volatility Index (VIX), often called the "fear gauge." The VIX measures the market's expectation of 30-day volatility.

If you believe the market is becoming too complacent and a period of turbulence is ahead, you could buy VIX futures or call options. If a market shock occurs and volatility spikes, the value of the VIX will soar, and your derivative position will become highly profitable. This can act as a powerful hedge, as VIX typically moves inversely to the stock market. When stocks fall, volatility and the VIX rise, providing a cushion for your portfolio.

A variance swap is a more direct way to trade volatility. In this contract, two parties agree to exchange a pre-agreed, fixed variance rate for the actual, realized variance of an asset over a period. If you buy a variance swap, you are betting that the actual market choppiness will be greater than what was initially expected. If you're right, you receive a payout. These instruments are used by hedge funds and institutional investors to isolate and trade volatility as a distinct asset class, independent of the direction of the underlying market.

Achieving Targeted Risk Exposures

Derivatives are the ultimate tool for customization. Instead of being stuck with the risk profile of traditional assets, you can use derivatives to achieve a precise exposure. For example, a pension fund might need to increase its allocation to long-term bonds to match its liabilities but finds it impractical to buy the physical bonds. Instead, it can use interest rate swaps or futures to synthetically create the desired bond exposure, achieving its goal more quickly and cheaply.

Similarly, an investor might want to capture the performance of emerging markets but is wary of the associated currency risk. They can buy an equity index future on an emerging market index while simultaneously using currency forwards to hedge out the foreign exchange exposure. The result is a pure, targeted bet on the growth of those foreign companies without the currency gamble. This process of "unbundling" risks allows a manager to choose exactly which risks they want to take on and which they want to discard, leading to a more efficient and intentionally constructed portfolio.

The Role of Derivatives in Asset Allocation and Market Insights

Derivatives are indispensable in modern asset allocation and rebalancing. A large institutional fund with a target allocation of 60% stocks and 40% bonds needs to maintain that balance. If stocks rally, the portfolio might drift to 65% stocks. Selling stocks and buying bonds to rebalance can incur significant transaction costs and taxes. A much more efficient method is to use futures. The manager can simply sell stock index futures and buy bond futures to bring the portfolio's effective exposure back to the 60/40 target. This is faster, cheaper, and less disruptive than trading the underlying assets.

Furthermore, derivative markets are a rich source of information about market expectations. The pricing of options, for instance, reveals the market's collective view on the probability of future price movements. A high price for out-of-the-money put options on a stock index suggests traders are nervous and anticipate a downturn. The term structure of futures prices—the difference between near-term and long-term contracts—can indicate expectations about future interest rates or commodity prices. By analyzing these markets, investors can gain valuable insights into market sentiment and position their portfolios accordingly, turning derivative data into a strategic advantage.

Currency Management: An Introduction

Welcome to the intricate and fascinating world of currency management. For any global investor, understanding the ebb and flow of foreign exchange rates isn't just an academic exercise; it's a critical component of portfolio survival and success. Currencies are the connective tissue of the global financial system, and their movements can either supercharge your returns or quietly erode your gains. This introduction will guide you through the essential concepts, from analyzing risk to implementing sophisticated hedging strategies.

Analyze the Effects of Currency Movements on Portfolio Risk and Return

Imagine you're a U.S.-based investor and you've bought shares in a fantastic German engineering company. The stock does brilliantly, soaring 10% in a year, measured in euros. You're ready to celebrate. But hold on. During that same year, the euro weakened by 8% against the U.S. dollar. When you convert your euro-denominated profits back into dollars, your actual return is much smaller, closer to just 2%. This simple scenario perfectly captures the dual nature of currency movements.

Currency fluctuations introduce an entirely separate layer of risk and potential return to an international portfolio. The total return of a foreign asset in your home currency is a combination of two things: the asset's local return and the percentage change in the foreign currency's value.

This can be expressed as:
$RDC \approx RFC + RFX$

where RDC is the total return in your domestic currency, RFC is the asset's return in its local foreign currency, and RFX is the return of the foreign currency relative to your domestic one.

This added dimension, the RFX component, increases the overall volatility (risk) of your portfolio. A key insight is that this currency risk is often considered "uncompensated." While you expect a positive return for taking on stock market risk, there's no inherent theoretical reason to expect a positive long-term return just from holding a foreign currency. It wiggles up and down, adding turbulence to your portfolio's journey without necessarily pushing it towards a better destination. Therefore, managing this volatility becomes a central question for any global investor.

Discuss Strategic Choices in Currency Management

When faced with currency risk, a portfolio manager has to make a fundamental, high-level decision. This isn't about day-to-day trading; it's about establishing a core philosophy. The strategic choices generally fall along a spectrum, from complete risk avoidance to actively seeking profits from currency moves.

Passive Hedging: This strategy aims to eliminate currency risk entirely. The manager will typically hedge 100% of the foreign currency exposure back to their domestic currency. The goal here is simple: isolate the return of the underlying foreign assets (the stocks and bonds) and remove the unpredictable noise from currency fluctuations. This is a conservative approcch, often favored by investors who believe their skill is in picking assets, not currencies.

Active Management: On the opposite end of the spectrum, this strategy treats currency as its own asset class, a potential source of alpha (excess returns). Managers who follow this path believe they can successfully forecast currency movements. They will take deliberate, unhedged positions, or even over-hedge, to profit from anticipated changes in exchange rates. This is a high-conviction strategy that transforms currency management from a defensive task into an offensive one.

Selective or Discretionary Hedging: This is the middle ground and perhaps the most common approach. The manager starts with a baseline policy, such as hedging 50% of the exposure (a neutral "beta" hedge). From there, they are given the discretion to deviate within a set range—for example, moving the hedge ratio between 25% and 75%. This allows them to express a view on a currency (by under-hedging if they think it will rise) without making an enormous, all-or-nothing bet. This approach blends risk reduction with opportunistic return-seeking.

Formulate an Appropriate Currency Management Program

Creating a currency management program is about translating a high-level strategy into a workable, disciplined plan. It's about building a framework that aligns with the portfolio's specific goals and limitations. There is no single "best" program; the right one depends entirely on the investor's unique situation.

The first step is to consider the portfolio's objectives and constraints. A pension fund with long-term, inflation-linked liabilities will have a very different risk tolerance than a hedge fund seeking short-term absolute returns. Key questions to ask include: What is our primary goal—risk reduction or alpha generation? What is our tolerance for short-term losses? How much are we willing to spend on hedging costs?

Once the philosophy is set, the practical steps follow:

Define the Benchmark: What is our neutral position? For a passive hedger, the benchmark is a 100% hedged portfolio. For an active manager, it might be an unhedged portfolio. This benchmark is the yardstick against which the program's success will be measured.

Set the Hedge Ratio: Based on the strategy, a target hedge ratio is established. This could be 0%, 50%, 100%, or any other level.

Establish Permitted Deviations: If active or selective hedging is chosen, clear tramlines must be put in place. For instance, the policy might state a target hedge of 50% with a tactical band of +/- 25%. This prevents a single manager from taking on excessive, unapproved risk.

Select Hedging Instruments: The program must specify which tools (e.g., forwards, futures, options) are permitted for implementing the hedges. This ensures transparency and control over the types of risks being taken.

Compare Active Currency Trading Strategies

For managers who choose to actively trade currencies, several distinct schools of thought guide their decisions. Each approach uses different information and operates on different time horizons.

Economic Fundamentals: This is a top-down approach focused on the big picture. Traders analyze macroeconomic factors to determine a currency's "fair value." They look at things like interest rate differentials (money flows to where it earns a higher return), inflation rates, GDP growth, and a country's balance of payments. For example, a country with high real interest rates and strong economic growth might be expected to have an appreciating currency. This strategy is often long-term in nature.

Technical Analysis: This approach completely ignores economic news and fundamentals. Instead, it focuses on one thing: price charts. Technical analysts believe that all known information is already reflected in the price and that historical patterns tend to repeat. They use tools like moving averages, trend lines, and momentum indicators to identify buy or sell signals. It's a strategy based on market psychology and flow, often used for shorter-term trading decisions.

Carry Trade: This is a very popular strategy that seeks to profit from interest rate differentials. The concept is simple: borrow a currency with a very low interest rate (like the Japanese Yen for many years) and use those funds to buy a currency with a high interest rate (like the Australian Dollar). The trader aims to pocket the difference, or "carry." The major risk is that the exchange rate moves against you, wiping out your interest rate gains. This strategy is profitable in low-volatility environments but can suffer catastrophic losses during "risk-off" panics.

Volatility Trading: This is a more sophisticated strategy that doesn't bet on the direction of a currency, but rather on how much it will move. Using options, a trader can structure a position that profits if volatility increases (a long straddle or strangle) or if it decreases (a short straddle or strangle). For instance, if a trader expects a central bank announcement to cause a huge currency swing but is unsure of the direction, they could buy volatility.

Describe How Changes in Factors Underlying Active Trading Strategies Affect Tactical Trading Decisions

Tactical decisions are the real-time adjustments made in response to new information. The specific factors that trigger these decisions depend entirely on the manager's chosen strategy.

For a fundamental trader, a tactical shift is driven by a change in the economic outlook. If the European Central Bank signals an unexpected interest rate hike, it changes the forecast for the euro's value. The trader must then decide whether to increase their long euro position or close it out. Similarly, a surprisingly weak inflation report could cause them to sell a currency they previously favored.

A technical trader, on the other hand, reacts to price action. Their tactical trigger isn't a news headline but a signal from their charts. If a currency pair breaks below a long-term moving average or a key support level, they might tactically decide to close a long position and even go short, regardless of the economic news. Their decisions are purely rule-based and systematic.

For a carry trader, the key factors are interest rate differentials and market risk appetite. A tactical decision to unwind a carry trade might be triggered if a central bank cuts rates in the high-yielding country, narrowing the profitable spread. More importantly, a sudden spike in global market fear (a "risk-off" event) is a massive red flag, as investors often flee high-yielding currencies for safe havens, causing sharp reversals that can quickly destroy a carry trade's profitability.

Finally, a volatility trader adjusts their position based on changes in expected market turbulence. If implied volatility (the market's forecast of future movement, priced into options) becomes very cheap, they may tactically decide to buy options, betting that a quiet market is about to get choppy.

Describe How Forward Contracts and FX Swaps Are Used to Adjust Hedge Ratios

Forward contracts and FX swaps are the workhorses of currency hedging. They are simple, efficient tools used to lock in exchange rates and manage currency exposures.

A forward contract is a straightforward agreement to buy or sell a specific amount of a foreign currency on a future date at a price agreed upon today. It's the most direct way to implement a hedge. Let's say a U.S. portfolio holds €10 million in assets and the manager wants a 75% hedge ratio. They would simply enter into a forward contract to sell €7.5 million (75% of the exposure) for U.S. dollars at a future date. This locks in the exchange rate for that portion of the portfolio, effectively removing the currency risk. If the manager wants to tactically adjust the hedge ratio to 60%, they can either partially close the existing forward or enter a new, smaller one.

An FX swap is slightly more complex but extremely common for rolling over existing hedges. It's a two-part transaction: an exchange of two currencies at the current spot rate, and an agreement to reverse that exchange at a future date at the forward rate. An FX swap is not used to create a new hedge but to manage the timing of cash flows from an existing one. For example, if a manager has a one-month forward hedge that is about to expire but they want to maintain the hedge for another month, they can use an FX swap to simultaneously settle the old position and establish a new one. This is often more cost-effective and operationally simpler than letting the old forward expire and then executing a brand new one.

Describe Trading Strategies Used to Reduce Hedging Costs and Modify Risk–Return Characteristics

While forwards provide a perfect hedge, they also come with an opportunity cost: if the foreign currency strengthens, you miss out on those gains. Furthermore, hedging isn't free. Several strategies can be used to lower these costs and reshape the portfolio's risk profile.

The most common tools for this are currency options. Unlike a forward contract, which is an obligation to transact, an option provides the right, but not the obligation, to do so.

Buying a Put Option: To protect against a foreign currency falling, a manager can buy a put option. This sets a floor for the exchange rate. If the currency weakens past the option's strike price, the option pays out, protecting the portfolio. If the currency strengthens, the manager can let the option expire worthless (losing only the premium paid) and benefit from the currency's appreciation. This provides downside protection with upside potential, but it comes at a cost—the option premium.

Zero-Cost Collar: To avoid paying the premium for an option, a manager can use a "collar." This involves buying a put option for downside protection and simultaneously selling a call option to finance it. The premium received from selling the call option can offset the cost of buying the put. The trade-off is that by selling the call, the manager gives up any potential gains if the currency appreciates beyond the call's strike price. The portfolio is now "collared" within a specific range of exchange rates—

protected from big losses but also capped from enjoying big gains. This strategy modifies the risk-return profile by trimming both tails of the distribution.

Describe the Use of Cross-Hedges, Macro-Hedges, and Minimum-Variance-Hedge Ratios

Hedging a portfolio with exposure to dozens of currencies one-by-one can be inefficient and costly. More sophisticated techniques are needed for these complex situations.

Cross-Hedges: This strategy is used when a direct hedge is unavailable or too expensive, which is often the case for exotic or illiquid currencies. The idea is to hedge the exposure using a different, highly correlated currency that is more liquid and cheaper to trade. For example, if you have exposure to the Polish Zloty but find the forward market for it is thin, you might notice that it moves very closely with the euro. You could then place a cross-hedge by selling the euro as a proxy. It's an imperfect hedge, as the correlation can break down, but it's often a pragmatic and cost-effective solution.

Macro-Hedges: Rather than hedging every single currency exposure, a macro-hedge takes a big-picture view. The manager analyzes the portfolio's total, aggregate sensitivity to a major currency factor, like the U.S. Dollar Index (DXY). If the analysis shows the entire portfolio tends to lose value when the dollar strengthens, the manager can place a single, large hedge—for instance, by shorting DXY futures—to neutralize this overarching risk factor. This simplifies the hedging process dramatically.

Minimum-Variance-Hedge Ratio (MVHR): This is a quantitative approach to find the optimal hedge ratio that will result in the lowest possible portfolio volatility. The 100% hedge is not always the best from a risk-minimization standpoint, especially if the currency movements are correlated with the asset returns. The MVHR is calculated based on the volatility of the asset, the volatility of the currency, and the correlation between them. The formula is:

$$MVHR=\rho(RFC,RFX)\times\sigma RFX\sigma RFC$$

This tells you the precise hedge ratio that wil minimize the variance of your total return. It is a more statistically refined approach than simply picking an arbitrary hedge ratio.

Discuss Challenges for Managing Emerging Market Currency Exposures

Managing currency exposures in emerging markets (EM) presents a unique and formidable set of challenges that don't exist in developed markets. These currencies can offer high returns but come with commensurately high risks.

High Volatility and Political Risk: EM currencies are notoriously volatile. They can experience massive swings in a very short period due to political instability, changes in government policy, or sudden shifts in investor sentiment.

Low Liquidity and High Transaction Costs: Many EM currency markets are thin. It can be difficult to execute large trades without significantly moving the price against you. This lack of liquidity leads to much wider bid-ask spreads, making hedging far more expensive than in markets like the EUR/USD.

Capital Controls: This is a huge risk. An EM government can suddenly impose controls that restrict or prohibit investors from converting the local currency back into their home currency. Your money can get trapped, regardless of how well your investment has performed.

Contagion Risk: Emerging markets are often bundled together in the minds of global investors. A crisis in one country, say Turkey, can trigger a wave of panic selling across completely unrelated markets in Latin America or Asia. Your exposure can suffer due to events happening halfway around the world.

Lack of Reliable Hedging Instruments: For many smaller EM currencies, a deep and liquid market for long-dated forward contracts or options simply doesn't exist. This makes it incredibly difficult to implement a systematic, long-term hedging program, forcing managers to rely on less perfect cross-hedges or leave the exposure unhedged.

Ethical and Professional Standards

Code of Ethics and Standards of Professional Conduct

A Guide to the CFA Code of Ethics and Standards of Professional Conduct

The CFA Institute holds its members and candidates to the highest ethical standards in the global investment profession. This commitment is embodied in the Code of Ethics and Standards of Professional Conduct, a comprehensive framework that guides individuals in prioritizing client interests and maintaining public trust. Understanding this framework involves two key parts: knowing the disciplinary process that enforces these rules and deeply understanding the ethical responsibilities themselves.

The Structure of the Professional Conduct Program and Disciplinary Process

The CFA Institute Professional Conduct Program (PCP) is the mechanism through which the Code and Standards are enforced. It's a confidential and thorough process designed to be fair to all parties involved while protecting the integrity of the CFA designation. The entire process is based on the principles of self-regulation, which means the profession polices itself to maintain high standards.

The process begins when the Professional Conduct staff receives information about a potential violation. This can come from various sources, such as a self-disclosure by a member or candidate (which is required), a written complaint from a client or colleague, media reports, or even through proctors reporting suspicious behavior during an exam.

Once a potential violation is identified, the Professional Conduct staff initiates an inquiry. They will gather evidence, which might include requesting written explanations from the individual involved, interviewing all relevant parties, and collecting documents. The individual under review is given every opportunity to present their side of the story and provide their own evidence.

After the investigation, the staff makes a determination. There are a few possible outcomes at this stage. They might conclude that no violation occurred, in which case the matter is closed. They might decide to issue a cautionary letter, which is a private warning for minor issues, reminding the individual of their ethical obligations without imposing a formal sanction.

However, if the evidence suggests a violation did occur, the Professional Conduct staff will propose a disciplinary sanction. This proposed sanction is sent to the individual, who then has a choice. They can either accept the proposed sanction or reject it.

If the individual accepts the sanction, the matter is concluded. The sanctions can range in severity, from a private reprimand to a suspension of the right to use the CFA designation and membership in the CFA Institute, or even a permanent revocation. The specific sanction depends on the seriousness of the violation.

If the individual rejects the proposed sanction, the matter is escalated to a hearing panel composed of volunteer members of the Disciplinary Review Committee (DRC). These panelists are all CFA charterholders with significant industry experience. The panel reviews all the evidence from the initial investigation and hears arguments from both the Professional Conduct staff and the individual under review. After deliberating, the panel makes its own independent decision and may impose a sanction. This hearing process ensures that every case is reviewed by a panel of peers, adding a crucial layer of fairness and expert judgment to the process.

The Ethical Responsibilities of the Code and Standards

The Code of Ethics and Standards of Professional Conduct are the bedrock of ethical behavior for investment professionals. The Code is a set of broad principles, while the Standards provide specific, mandatory rules of conduct.

The Code of Ethics

The Code of Ethics is a pledge that all CFA members and candidates must adhere to. It establishes the core ethical principles of the profession and includes six key points:

Act with integrity, competence, diligence, and respect in an ethical manner with the public, clients, prospective clients, employers, employees, colleagues, and other participants in the global capital markets.

Place the integrity of the investment profession and the interests of clients above their own personal interests. This is the cornerstone of the entire ethical framework.

Use reasonable care and exercise independent professional judgment when conducting investment analysis, making investment recommendations, taking investment actions, and engaging in other professional activities.

Practice and encourage others to practice in a professional and ethical manner that will reflect credit on themselves and the profession.

Promote the integrity and viability of the global capital markets for the ultimate benefit of society.

Maintain and improve their professional competence and strive to maintain and improve the competence of other investment professionals.

The Standards of Professional Conduct

The seven Standards of Professional Conduct break down the principles of the Code into actionable rules.

I. Professionalism: This standard focuses on the overall integrity of your conduct.

Knowledge of the Law: You must understand and comply with all applicable laws, rules, and regulations. If there's a conflict between different laws or regulations, you must follow the more strict one. You cannot knowingly participate in or assist in any violation.

Independence and Objectivity: You must use reasonable care and judgment to achieve and maintain independence and objectivity. You must not offer, solicit, or accept any gift or compensation that could compromise your own or another's independence.

Misrepresentation: You cannot knowingly make any misrepresentations related to investment analysis, recommendations, or other professional activities. This includes plagiarism.

Misconduct: You must not engage in any professional conduct involving dishonesty, fraud, or deceit or commit any act that reflects adversely on your professional reputation, integrity, or competence.

II. Integrity of Capital Markets: This standard is about maintaining a fair and honest marketplace.

Material Nonpublic Information: If you possess material nonpublic information that could affect the value of an investment, you cannot act on it or cause others to act on it.

Market Manipulation: You must not engage in practices that distort prices or artificially inflate trading volume with the intent to mislead market participants.

III. Duties to Clients: This is a crucial standard centered on client relationships.

Loyalty, Prudence, and Care: You have a duty of loyalty to your clients and must act with reasonable care and exercise prudent judgment. You must always place your clients' interests before your employer's or your own.

Fair Dealing: You must deal fairly and objectively with all clients when providing investment analysis, making recommendations, or taking investment action.

Suitability: When you are in an advisory relationship, you must make a reasonable inquiry into a client's investment experience, risk and return objectives, and financial constraints. You must then ensure that any investment action is suitable for their situation and consistent with their written objectives.

Performance Presentation: When communicating investment performance information, you must make reasonable efforts to ensure that it is fair, accurate, and complete.

Preservation of Confidentiality: You must keep information about current, former, and prospective clients confidential unless the information concerns illegal activities, disclosure is required by law, or the client permits disclosure.

IV. Duties to Employers: This outlines your responsibilities to the firm you work for.

Loyalty: In matters related to your employment, you must act for the benefit of your employer and not deprive them of your skills, divulge confidential information, or otherwise cause harm to your employer.

Additional Compensation Arrangements: You must not accept gifts or benefits that compete with or might create a conflict of interest with your employer's interest unless you get written consent from all parties involved.

Responsibilities of Supervisors: If you supervise others, you must make reasonable efforts to ensure that anyone subject to your supervision complies with applicable laws, regulations, and the Code and Standards.

V. Investment Analysis, Recommendations, and Actions: This focuses on the quality of your work.

Diligence and Reasonable Basis: Your investment analysis and recommendations must have a reasonable and adequate basis, supported by appropriate research and investigation.

Communication with Clients and Prospective Clients: You must disclose the basic format and general principles of the investment processes you use. You must also disclose significant limitations and risks.

Record Retention: You must develop and maintain appropriate records to support your investment analysis and recommendations.

VI. Conflicts of Interest: This standard requires you to be transparent about potential conflicts.

Disclosure of Conflicts: You must make full and fair disclosure of all matters that could impair your independence and objectivity or interfere with your duties to clients or your employer.

Priority of Transactions: Investment transactions for clients and employers must have priority over your own personal transactions.

Referral Fees: You must disclose to your employer and to clients any compensation you receive for the recommendation of products or services.

VII. Responsibilities as a CFA Institute Member or CFA Candidate: This covers your obligations to the CFA Institute itself.

Conduct as Participants in CFA Institute Programs: You must not engage in any conduct that compromises the reputation or integrity of the CFA Institute or the CFA designation or the integrity, validity, or security of the CFA exams.

Reference to CFA Institute, the CFA Designation, and the CFA Program: When referring to your status, you must not misrepresent or exaggerate the meaning or implications of membership in CFA Institute or holding the CFA designation.

Guidance for Standards I-VII

Guidance for Standards I–VII: A Comprehensive Overview

The CFA Institute Code of Ethics and Standards of Professional Conduct form the ethical backbone of the investment profession. Adherence to these principles is paramount for building trust, maintaining the integrity of capital markets, and always putting the client's interests first. This guide provides a thorough exploration of Standards I through VII, offering interpretations for various real-world scenarios and recommending practices to prevent violations.

Standard I: Professionalism

Standard I is the bedrock upon which a C-level executive's reputation is built. It encompasses a deep knowledge of the law, the importance of independence and objectivity, the dangers of misrepresentation, and the gravity of misconduct.

A thorough knowledge of the law is not just about avoiding legal trouble; it's about understanding the complex web of regulations that govern the financial industry. For a C-level executive, this means staying current on securities laws, tax regulations, and any industry-specific rules that apply to their firm. Imagine a scenario where a company is considering a merger. The CEO must be aware of antitrust laws to ensure the deal doesn't create an unfair market advantage. A violation could lead to hefty fines and reputational damage. To prevent this, executives should consult with legal counsel early and often, foster a culture of compliance within the organization, and invest in ongoing training for all employees.

Independence and objectivity are the cornerstones of trust. A C-level executive must be free from any influence that could compromise their judgment. Consider a Chief Financial Officer (CFO) who is offered a lavish trip by a potential underwriter for the company's upcoming IPO. Accepting this gift could create the appearance of a conflict of interest, even if the CFO believes they can remain objective. The best practice here is to have a clear and strict gift policy that applies to everyone in the company. All gifts, no matter how small, should be disclosed, and anything that could be perceived as a bribe should be politely declined.

Misrepresentation is a poison that can erode trust in an instant. This standard is not just about outright lies; it's also about omitting crucial information or presenting data in a misleading way. A Chief Marketing Officer (CMO), for instance, might be tempted to exaggerate a product's performance in an advertising campaign. While this might lead to a short-term sales boost, the long-term consequences of misleading customers can be devastating. To avoid this, C-level executives must instill a commitment to transparency and accuracy in all communications. All claims should be backed by verifiable data, and any potential risks or limitations should be clearly disclosed.

Finally, misconduct, in any form, is unacceptable. This includes any behavior that reflects poorly on the executive's professional reputation, integrity, or competence. A Chief Technology Officer (CTO) who engages in insider trading, for example, is not only breaking the law but also betraying the trust of shareholders and the public. To prevent misconduct, companies should have a robust code of conduct that is regularly reviewed and enforced. There should be clear consequences for violations, and a system in place for employees to report unethical behavior without fear of retaliation.

Standard II: Integrity of Capital Markets

The integrity of capital markets is the engine that drives economic growth. When investors have confidence that the markets are fair and transparent, they are more willing to risk their capital, which in turn funds innovation and creates jobs. Standard II is dedicated to preserving this trust by prohibiting the use of material nonpublic information and market manipulation.

Material nonpublic information, often referred to as inside information, is any information that could reasonably be expected to affect a security's price that has not yet been made public. Using this information to make a personal profit or to help someone else do so is a serious breach of trust and, in most cases, illegal. Imagine a CEO who learns that their company is about to be acquired at a significant premium. If they were to buy shares of their company's stock before the news is announced, they would be engaging in insider trading. The consequences of this can be severe, including fines, imprisonment, and a permanent ban from the securities industry.

To prevent the misuse of material nonpublic information, companies must have strict policies in place. These should include a "firewall" between departments that have access to sensitive information and those that do not. There should also be a clear "need-to-know" policy, meaning that only employees who require the information to do their jobs should have access to it. Additionally, companies should maintain a "restricted list" of securities that employees are prohibited from trading.

Market manipulation is a broad term that covers a range of activities designed to distort securities prices or trading volume. This can include spreading false rumors to drive a stock's price down, or engaging in a series of trades to create the illusion of high demand. For example, a group of traders might conspire to buy and sell a thinly traded stock among themselves to create the appearance of activity and lure in unsuspecting investors. This is a classic "pump and dump" scheme.

To prevent market manipulation, firms should have robust surveillance systems in place to monitor trading activity for any unusual patterns. They should also provide training to employees on how to identify and report suspicious behavior. Regulators also play a crucial role in policing the markets and bringing enforcement actions against those who engage in manipulative practices.
Standard III: Duties to Clients

The relationship between an investment professional and their client is a fiduciary one, meaning it is built on a foundation of trust and confidence. Standard III outlines the duties that professionals owe to their clients, which include loyalty, prudence, and care; fair dealing; suitability; performance presentation; and preservation of confidentiality.

Loyalty, prudence, and care are the three pillars of this standard. Loyalty means that the client's interests must always come before the professional's. Prudence means that the professional must act with the same level of care and skill as a reasonable person would in a similar situation. Care means that the professional must have a thorough understanding of the client's financial situation, goals, and risk tolerance.

Fair dealing requires that all clients be treated equitably. This doesn't mean that all clients must have the same portfolio, but it does mean that no client should be given preferential treatment over another. For example, if a portfolio manager has a hot stock tip, they cannot just give it to their largest clients. They must have a system in place to disseminate the information to all clients in a fair and timely manner.

Suitability is the cornerstone of ethical investment advice. Before making any recommendation, a professional must make a reasonable inquiry into a client's investment experience, risk and return objectives, and financial constraints. The investment must be suitable for the client's specific situation. For example, it would be unsuitable to recommend a high-risk venture capital investment to a retiree who is living on a fixed income.

Performance presentation is another area where professionals must be scrupulously honest. When presenting performance data, professionals must make every effort to ensure that it is fair, accurate, and complete. This means not cherry-picking the best-performing accounts or using misleading benchmarks. It also means disclosing any fees or expenses that could impact a client's returns.

Finally, preservation of confidentiality is a sacred trust. Professionals have access to a great deal of sensitive information about their clients, and they have a duty to keep this information confidential. This includes not only financial information but also personal details. The only time it is acceptable to disclose client information is with the client's permission or when required by law.

Standard IV: Duties to Employers

While the duty to clients is paramount, professionals also have a duty to their employers. Standard IV outlines these responsibilities, which include loyalty, additional compensation arrangements, and responsibilities of supervisors.

Loyalty to an employer means acting in their best interest and not doing anything that would harm the company. This includes not competing with the employer, not soliciting the employer's clients for personal gain, and not disclosing confidential information. For example, an employee who is planning to leave a firm to start their own business cannot take the firm's client list with them.

Additional compensation arrangements can create conflicts of interest, so they must be handled with care. If an employee is offered compensation or benefits from a third party that could create a conflict of interest with their employer's interest, they must disclose it to their employer in writing. For example, if a research analyst is offered a paid trip by a company they cover, they must get their employer's permission before accepting it.

Responsibilities of supervisors are a critical part of this standard. Supervisors have a duty to ensure that the employees they oversee comply with all applicable laws, rules, regulations, and the firm's own policies and procedures. This means having a robust compliance program in place, providing adequate training, and taking prompt action to correct any violations. A supervisor who turns a blind eye to unethical behavior by their subordinates can be held just as responsible as the employees who committed the violation.

Standard V: Investment Analysis, Recommendations, and Actions

Standard V focuses on the integrity of the investment decision-making process. It requires that professionals have a reasonable basis for their investment recommendations, that they communicate their investment analysis in a clear and transparent way, and that they maintain records to support their decisions.

Diligence and a reasonable basis are the starting point for any sound investment recommendation. This means conducting a thorough investigation of the investment, considering all relevant factors, and documenting the research process. For example, before recommending a stock, an analyst should review the company's financial statements, analyze its competitive position, and assess the quality of its management team.

Communication with clients and prospective clients is also critical. Professionals must distinguish between fact and opinion in their research reports and recommendations. They should also disclose the basic formats and general principles of the investment processes they use to analyze investments, select securities, and construct portfolios. This allows clients to make informed decisions about whether to follow the professional's advice.

Record retention is a key part of this standard. Professionals must develop and maintain appropriate records to support their investment analysis, recommendations, and actions. This documentation can be critical in the event of a dispute with a client or a regulatory investigation.

Standard VI: Conflicts of Interest

Conflicts of interest are a fact of life in the investment profession. The key is to manage them in a way that is fair and transparent. Standard VI requires that professionals disclose any potential conflicts of interest to clients, prospects, and their employer. It also has specific rules regarding referral fees and giving priority to client transactions over personal transactions.

Disclosure of conflicts is the most important part of this standard. Professionals must make full and fair disclosure of all matters that could reasonably be expected to impair their independence and objectivity or interfere with their duties to clients, prospects, or their employer. For example, if a portfolio manager owns stock in a company that they are recommending to clients, they must disclose this to the clients.

Priority of transactions is another key area. Client transactions must always take precedence over personal transactions. This means that professionals cannot trade on their own account ahead of a client's order. This is known as "front-running" and is a serious violation of this standard.

Referral fees must also be disclosed. If a professional receives any compensation for recommending a product or service to a client, they must disclose this to the client. This allows the client to assess whether the recommendation is truly in their best interest or if it is being influenced by the referral fee.

Standard VII: Responsibilities as a CFA Institute Member or CFA Candidate

The final standard, Standard VII, applies to all CFA Institute members and candidates. It requires them to conduct themselves in a way that does not compromise the reputation or integrity of the CFA Institute or the CFA designation. It also prohibits any conduct that would be considered a violation of the Code and Standards.

Conduct as participants in CFA Institute programs is a key part of this standard. This includes not cheating on exams, not disclosing confidential exam information, and not engaging in any other conduct that would compromise the integrity of the CFA Program.

Reference to CFA Institute, the CFA designation, and the CFA Program must also be done in a professional and appropriate manner. Members and candidates cannot misrepresent their status in the program or make any promises or guarantees that are tied to the CFA designation.

In conclusion, the CFA Institute Code of Ethics and Standards of Professional Conduct provide a comprehensive framework for ethical decision-making in the investment profession. By understanding and applying these principles, professionals can build a career that is not only successful but also one they can be proud of.

Application of the Code and Standards: Level III

Applying the CFA Institute Code and Standards: A Level III Perspective

Navigating the ethical landscape of the investment profession requires more than just knowing the rules; it demands a sophisticated ability to analyze complex situations and make sound judgments. For a CFA Level III candidate, this means moving beyond simple recognition of violations to a deeper level of evaluation. It involves dissecting practices, policies, and individual conduct to determine their alignment with the CFA Institute Code of Ethics and Standards of Professional Conduct. This guide explores the nuanced process of evaluating ethical dilemmas and clearly articulating whether a specific action constitutes a violation.

Evaluating Practices, Policies, and Conduct

At its core, evaluating conduct against the Code and Standards is a methodical process of inquiry and analysis. It's about looking at a situation not just for what happened, but for the principles that were upheld or compromised. This requires a shift from a black-and-white perspective to one that appreciates the gray areas where ethical challenges often reside. The goal is to develop a framework for thinking that can be applied consistently to any scenario, whether it involves a complex portfolio management strategy, a firm-wide policy, or a casual conversation with a client.

The first step in any evaluation is to gather all the relevant facts. Who was involved? What actions were taken? When and where did this occur? What were the motivations and outcomes? It's crucial to avoid jumping to conclusions based on incomplete information. A seemingly unethical act might be perfectly acceptable when viewed in its full context. For instance, a portfolio manager selling a particular stock from all client accounts could be seen as a violation of suitability standards. However, if new research revealed a fundamental flaw in the company's business model, that same action becomes a demonstration of diligence and loyalty to clients.

Once the facts are established, the next step is to identify which specific Standards of Professional Conduct might apply. This is where a deep understanding of the Standards becomes essential. The seven main standards—Professionalism; Integrity of Capital Markets; Duties to Clients; Duties to Employers; Investment Analysis, Recommendations, and Actions; Conflicts of Interest; and Responsibilities as a CFA Institute Member or CFA Candidate—cover a vast range of professional activities. A single scenario can often touch upon multiple standards. For example, an analyst who fails to disclose a personal ownership stake in a company they are recommending is not only dealing with a Conflict of Interest but is also potentially violating their duties of Loyalty to their employer and Independence and Objectivity.

With the relevant standards identified, the heart of the evaluation begins: a critical assessment of the conduct in question. This involves asking a series of probing questions. Did the individual or firm act with integrity, competence, and diligence? Was their conduct fair and respectful to all parties? Did they place the integrity of the investment profession and the interests of clients above their own personal interests? This part of the process requires you to think like an ethicist, weighing the principles behind the rules.

Consider a firm-wide policy that restricts personal trading for all employees. To evaluate this policy, you would look at its purpose. Is it designed to prevent employees from front-running client trades, a clear violation of the Standard related to Material Nonpublic Information? Or is it so restrictive that it unfairly limits the ability of employees to manage their own financial affairs, potentially creating a conflict with their Duties to their Employer? A good policy will strike a balance, effectively mitigating risk without being overly burdensome.

Evaluating individual conduct often involves more nuance. Imagine a portfolio manager who uses a "soft dollar" arrangement, where brokerage commissions are used to pay for research services. This practice is not inherently a violation. The evaluation hinges on the details. Does the research benefit the clients whose commissions are paying for it? Is the research substantive and does it contribute to the investment decision-making process? If the soft dollars are being used to pay for the manager's office rent or a vacation, it's a clear violation of their Duty of Loyalty to clients. The evaluation is not about the practice itself, but about how it is applied.

Ultimately, this level of evaluation is about connecting actions back to fundamental ethical principles. The Code and Standards are not just a list of prohibitions; they are a framework for building trust. When you evaluate a practice, policy, or individual action, you are essentially asking: Does this build or erode trust with clients, employers, and the market as a whole?

Articulating Violations of the Code and Standards

Being able to identify an ethical violation is only half the battle. A Level III candidate must also be able to clearly and concisely explain how and why a particular action violates the CFA Institute Code of Ethics and Standards of Professional Conduct. This skill is critical not only for the exam but for real-world professional practice, where you may need to justify a decision to a client, a supervisor, or a regulatory body. A well-reasoned explanation demonstrates a mastery of the material and a commitment to ethical conduct.

The key to a successful explanation is to be specific. It is not enough to simply state, "This is a violation of the Code and Standards." You must connect the specific facts of the case to the specific language of the standards. This creates a logical bridge that leaves no room for ambiguity. Your explanation should follow a clear structure: state the conclusion, identify the relevant standard(s), and then meticulously link the conduct to the principles of that standard.

Let's begin with the conclusion. Start with a direct statement. For example, "John Doe's actions violated Standard IV(A), Loyalty." This immediately frames the discussion and tells your audience exactly where you stand. There is no need for a lengthy preamble; a clear, declarative sentence is most effective.

Next, you must identify the relevant standard by its number and name. Citing "Standard IV(A), Loyalty" is more precise than saying "the standard about loyalty to employers." Precision is a hallmark of professionalism. In your explanation, it's often helpful to briefly summarize the core principle of the standard. For Standard IV(A), Loyalty, you might say, "This standard requires members and candidates to act for the benefit of their employer and not deprive their employer of the advantage of their skills and abilities, divulge confidential information, or otherwise cause harm to their employer."

The most critical part of the explanation is the application of the facts to the standard. This is where you build your case. You need to draw a direct line from the person's conduct to the requirements of the standard they have violated. Use the facts you've gathered to show, point by point, how the standard was breached.

Imagine a scenario where an analyst, Jane Smith, is preparing to leave her firm. Before resigning, she downloads a proprietary financial model she developed onto a personal flash drive. In your explanation of this violation, you would lay out the logic step-by-step. "Jane Smith's conduct is a clear violation of Standard IV(A), Loyalty. The standard obligates her to protect her employer's property and not misuse it for personal gain. The financial model, developed during her employment, is the property of her firm. By downloading the model for her own use after she leaves, she is misappropriating her employer's property. This action directly harms her employer by depriving them of a valuable asset she was paid to create."

Notice how this explanation connects the action (downloading the model) to the ownership of the model (firm property) and the specific obligation under the standard (not to misappropriate employer property). It also explains the consequence of the action—harm to the employer.

In many cases, an action will violate multiple standards. A strong explanation will address each violation separately. For instance, if an investment advisor promises a client a "guaranteed 15% return," this violates multiple standards. You would first explain the violation of Standard I(C), Misrepresentation. "The advisor violated Standard I(C) by misrepresenting the potential return on the investment. Investment returns are inherently uncertain, and guaranteeing a specific return is misleading to the client." Then, you would explain the violation of Standard III(A), Loyalty, Prudence, and Care. "By making an unrealistic promise, the advisor failed to act with the necessary care and prudence in their duty to the client. A prudent advisor would provide a realistic assessment of potential risks and returns, not a baseless guarantee."

Finally, a complete explanation often includes guidance on what the individual should have done. This demonstrates a constructive, forward-looking understanding of ethical practice. In the case of Jane Smith and the financial model, you might add, "To comply with Standard IV(A), Ms. Smith should have left all firm property, including any models or research she developed, with her employer upon her departure. If she wished to use her skills to recreate a similar model at a new firm, she could do so based on her knowledge and experience, without taking any of her previous employer's property." This not only solidifies your explanation of the violation but also reinforces the proper ethical conduct.

Asset Manager Code of Professional Conduct

The Purpose and Benefits of the Asset Manager Code

Think of the Asset Manager Code of Professional Conduct as a North Star for investment firms. In a world filled with complex financial instruments and fast-moving markets, it provides a simple, clear guide on how to do business the right way. Its primary purpose isn't just to list a bunch of rules; it's to build and protect the single most valuable asset in the financial industry: trust. Without trust, the entire system grinds to a halt. Clients won't invest their savings, and markets can't function efficiently. The Code provides a universal ethical benchmark that tells clients, regulators, and the public that a firm is committed to a higher standard.

The core idea is to create a culture where the client's interests are always placed first. It's a voluntary code, which makes a firm's decision to adopt it even more powerful. It's a public declaration that the firm vows to act with integrity, competence, and transparency. This isn't about finding loopholes or just meeting the bare minimum legal requirements. It's about striving for excellence in ethical conduct and ensuring that every decision, from a single trade to a long-term investment strategy, is made with the client's best interests at heart. It's a framework for professionalizing the industry from the inside out.

The benefits that flow to a firm that genuinely adopts the Code are immense and can be a game-changer. First and foremost, it becomes a powerful mark of distinction. In a crowded marketplace, being able to tell potential clients that you voluntarily adhere to the highest ethical standards in the industry is a significant competitive advantage. It builds confidence and can be the deciding factor for a high-net-worth individual or a large pension fund looking for a trustworthy steward of their capital.

Furthermore, it strengthens the firm internally. A strong ethical culture attracts and retains top talent. The best professionals want to work for organizations that they can be proud of, where they aren't pressured to bend the rules to make a quick profit. This reduces employee turnover and fosters a more stable, positive work environment. Finally, adopting the Code can lead to better relationships with regulators. By demonstrating a proactive commitment to self-regulation and ethical conduct, firms may be viewed more favorably, building a reservoir of goodwill that is invaluable in a heavily regulated industry. It is, in essence, an investment in the firm's long-term reputation and success.

The Six General Principles of Conduct Explained

The Asset Manager Code is built upon six foundational principles that guide a firm's responsibilities. These principles are not just abstract ideals; they are the pillars of ethical and professional behavior in the investment world.

1. Act in a professional and ethical manner at all times. This is the bedrock principle. It means conducting yourself with integrity, dignity, and honesty in every interaction. It's about more than just not breaking the law; it's about doing the right thing, even when no one is watching. This includes being truthful in your communications, honoring your commitments, and treating clients, colleagues, and competitors with respect. It's the promise that you will be a trustworthy professional in all your dealings.

2. Act for the benefit of clients.
This principle enshrines the concept of fiduciary duty. When a client entrusts you with their money, their interests must become your interests. You must place their financial well-being ahead of your own and ahead of your firm's. This means you cannot use their assets to benefit yourself, for example, by making trades in their account to generate higher commissions for your firm. Any potential conflict of interest must be avoided or, if unavoidable, fully disclosed to the client in a clear and understandable way.

3. Act with independence and objectivity.
Your investment advice and actions must be based on solid, unbiased research and your best professional judgment. You cannot let outside influences cloud your thinking. This means you can't accept lavish gifts or entertainment from a brokerage firm that might subtly influence you to direct more trades their way. Your decisions must be untainted by personal biases, conflicts of interest, or pressure from others. Your loyalty is to the client and the truth of your analysis, period.

4. Act with skill, competence, and diligence.
Managing assets requires expertise. This principle demands that you not only have the necessary knowledge and skills to do your job but that you also work hard to maintain and improve them. The financial world is constantly changing, so a commitment to lifelong learning is essential. It also means being thorough and careful in your work. Whether you are researching a stock or executing a trade, you must act with diligence—the same level of care that a prudent person would exercise in managing their own affairs.

5. Communicate with clients in a timely and accurate manner.
Communication is key to building trust. This principle requires you to be clear, honest, and prompt in all your communications with clients. You must provide them with information they can actually understand, avoiding overly technical jargon. This includes explaining your investment philosophy, the risks involved in their portfolio, the fees they are paying, and their performance. Importantly, this means delivering bad news with the same candor as good news.

6. Uphold the applicable rules governing capital markets.
Asset managers are key players in the global financial system. This principle recognizes that you have a responsibility to protect the integrity of the capital markets as a whole. This means you must know and obey all applicable laws and regulations, such as those prohibiting insider trading or market manipulation. By acting ethically, you help ensure that the markets are fair and efficient for all participants, which ultimately benefits everyone, including your clients.

Determining if a Firm's Practices are Consistent with the Code

Knowing the principles is one thing; living them is another. To determine if an asset manager's practices and procedures are truly consistent with the Code, you have to look beyond their marketing materials and dig into their day-to-day operations. It's an investigative process that focuses on actions, not just words.

A great starting point is to examine the firm's core documents. Is there a formal, written compliance manual that explicitly references the principles of the Asset Manager Code? This manual should be the firm's playbook, translating the high-level principles into concrete, real-world procedures. For example, under the principle of "acting for the benefit of clients," you would look for a detailed policy on how trades are allocated among different client accounts. A consistent firm will have a fair and transparent system, ensuring that no single client (like a large, profitable one) consistently gets better prices at the expense of others.

Next, you must assess the firm's culture, which often speaks louder than any manual. How does leadership talk about ethics? Is compliance seen as a partner in the business or as a roadblock to profits? You can gauge this by looking at the firm's training programs. Are they engaging, frequent, and focused on real-life ethical dilemmas, or are they a once-a-year, check-the-box formality? A firm that is truly consistent will have a "speak up" culture, where employees feel safe reporting potential ethical breaches without fear of retaliation.

Finally, you need to audit specific, high-risk areas. For instance, to check for "independence and objectivity," you would review the firm's policies on gifts and entertainment. Is there a clear, modest dollar limit? How are relationships with brokers evaluated? The decision to use a certain broker should be based on their ability to provide the best execution for the client, not on how many steak dinners they offer. Similarly, reviewing employee personal trading records can reveal whether they are front-running client trades—a clear violation. A firm consistent with the Code will have robust monitoring systems in place to catch these inconsistencies and demonstrate that their loyalty lies squarely with their clients.

Practices and Procedures to Prevent Violations

Preventing violations of the Asset Manager Code requires building a strong and resilient ethical infrastructure. It's not about having a single solution but about creating a multi-layered system designed to promote good behavior and catch problems before they escalate.

First and foremost, a firm must make a formal commitment. This begins with senior management formally adopting the Code and communicating its importance to every single employee. This commitment should be woven into the fabric of the firm. A crucial next step is to appoint a Chief Compliance Officer (CCO) who is experienced, well-resourced, and, critically, has the authority to enforce the rules. The CCO should report directly to the CEO or the board of directors, ensuring their independence is not compromised.

The next layer is documentation. A clear, comprehensive, and easy-to-understand compliance manual is non-negotiable. This manual must translate the Code's principles into specific, actionable policies. For example, instead of just saying "avoid conflicts of interest," the manual should have a detailed section on personal trading. It should require employees to pre-clear trades, hold investments for a minimum period, and submit regular statements of their holdings. It should also have a strict policy on gifts, setting a clear dollar limit to prevent judgment from being swayed.

Education is the third critical layer. You cannot expect employees to follow rules they don't understand. The firm must implement a mandatory and ongoing training program. This shouldn't be a boring lecture. Effective training uses real-world case studies to show how ethical dilemmas can arise in daily work and provides a clear framework for resolving them. A junior analyst, for example, should be trained on what to do if they overhear potentially material non-public information.

Finally, you need a system of verification and enforcement. This means "trust, but verify." The firm should implement robust monitoring and testing procedures. This includes regular reviews of trading activity to detect patterns of abuse, audits of marketing materials to ensure they are accurate and not misleading, and periodic testing of the compliance procedures themselves to see if they are working as designed. When a violation is detected, it must be addressed swiftly, fairly, and decisively. Taking clear action sends a powerful message that the Code is not just a piece of paper on the wall—it is the standard by which everyone at the firm is expected to live.

About Author

Azhar ul Haque Sario is a bestselling author and data scientist with a remarkable record of achievement. This Cambridge alumnus brings a wealth of knowledge to his work, holding an MBA, ACCA (Knowledge Level - FTMS College Malaysia and London College of Accountancy, London), BBA, and several Google certifications, including specializations in Google Data Analytics, Google Digital Marketing & E-commerce, and Google Project Management.

With ten years of business experience, Azhar combines practical expertise with his impressive academic background to craft insightful books. His prolific writing has resulted in an astounding 2810 published titles, earning him the record for the maximum Kindle editions and paperback books published by an individual author in one year, awarded by Asia Books of Records in 2024.

ORCID: https://orcid.org/0009-0004-8629-830X
Azhar.sario@hotmail.co.uk
https://www.linkedin.com/in/azharulhaquesario/

www.ingramcontent.com/pod-product-compliance
Lightning Source LLC
Chambersburg PA
CBHW031346230926
51848CB00002B/409
9783384731166